Churchill

THE PLAYWRIGHT

D0088593

In the same series

ARDEN: A STUDY OF HIS PLAYS
Albert Hunt

BECKETT THE PLAYWRIGHT
John Fletcher and John Spurling

BOND: A STUDY OF HIS PLAYS
Malcolm Hay and Philip Roberts

BRECHT: A CHOICE OF EVILS
Martin Esslin

COWARD THE PLAYWRIGHT
John Lahr

MILLER THE PLAYWRIGHT
Dennis Welland

ODETS THE PLAYWRIGHT
Gerald Weales

PINTER THE PLAYWRIGHT
Martin Esslin

STOPPARD THE PLAYWRIGHT
Michael Billington

WESKER THE PLAYWRIGHT
Glenda Leeming

Churchill

THE PLAYWRIGHT

Geraldine Cousin

METHUEN · DRAMA

A Methuen Paperback

First published in Great Britain in 1989
in simultaneous hardback and paperback editions
by Methuen Drama, Michelin House, 81 Fulham Road, London SW3 6RB
and distributed in the United States of America
by HEB Inc., 70 Court Street, Portemouth, New Hampshire 03801
Copyright © 1989 by Geraldine Cousin

British Library Cataloguing in Publication Data

Cousin, Geraldine
    Churchill, the playwright
    I. Title
    822′.914

    ISBN 0-413-61310-0
    ISBN 0-413-14790-8 Pbk

Photoset by Rowland Phototypesetting Ltd
Bury St Edmunds, Suffolk
Printed in Great Britain by
Richard Clay Ltd, Bungay, Suffolk

Contents

Acknowledgements

My thanks to David Lan for permission to quote from *A Mouthful of Birds*; Les Waters and Annie Smart for talking to me about *Fen* and *A Mouthful of Birds*; Max Stafford-Clark for allowing me to watch a number of rehearsals of *Serious Money*; Linda Fitzsimmons for help in compiling the Chronology; and, above all, to Caryl Churchill for loaning me unpublished scripts, and also notebooks for *Light Shining in Buckinghamshire*, *Cloud Nine* and *Fen*, allowing me to quote from her published and unpublished work, and for the constant patience and kindness with which she answered my many questions.

Illustrations

OWNERS: Royal Court Theatre Upstairs, London, 1972. Left to right: David Swift, Jill Bennett, Richard O'Callaghan. (Photo: John Haynes)

LIGHT SHINING IN BUCKINGHAMSHIRE: Royal Court Theatre Upstairs, London, 1976. Left to right: Robert Hamilton, Will Knightley, Nigel Terry, Linda Goddard, Colin McCormack, Carole Hayman. (Photo: John Haynes)

LIGHT SHINING IN BUCKINGHAMSHIRE: Royal Court Theatre Upstairs, London, 1976. Left to right: Will Knightley, Nigel Terry, Linda Goddard, Colin McCormack. (Photo: John Haynes)

CLOUD NINE: Royal Court Theatre, London 1979, rehearsal photograph. Left to right: William Hoyland, Julie Covington, Max Stafford-Clark (director). (Photo: Paul Roylance)

CLOUD NINE: revival at Royal Court Theatre, London, 1980. Maggie Steed as Mrs Saunders. (Photo: John Haynes)

CLOUD NINE: Royal Court Theatre, London, 1979. Left to right: Anthony Sher, Carole Hayman, Julile Covington. (Photo: John Haynes)

TOP GIRLS: Royal Court Theatre, London, 1982. Left to right: Lindsay Duncan, Carole Hayman, Gwen Taylor, Selina Cadell. (Photo: Catherine Ashmore)

TOP GIRLS: Royal Court Theatre, London 1982. Left to right: Lindsay Duncan, Carole Hayman. (Photo: Catherine Ashmore)

FEN: Almeida Theatre, London, 1983. Amelda Brown. (Photo: John Haynes)

A MOUTHFUL OF BIRDS: Birmingham Repertory Theatre, 1986. Left to right: Tricia Kelly, Christian Burgess. (Photo: Phil Cutts)

A MOUTHFUL OF BIRDS: Birmingham Repertory Theatre, 1986. Left to right: Stephen Goff, Philippe Giraudeau. (Photo: Phil Cutts)

SERIOUS MONEY: Second cast, Royal Court Theatre, London, 1987. (Photo: John Haynes)

Chronology of a Career

1938:   Born in London, 3 September.
1948–55: Lived in Montreal, Canada.
1957–60: Read English Language and Literature at Lady Margaret Hall, Oxford. Obtained B.A. in English.
1958:   Student production at Oxford of *Downstairs* (one-act play), which went to the *Sunday Times*/National Union of Students Drama Festival in 1959.
1960:   Student production of *Having a Wonderful Time* at The Questors Theatre, Ealing.
1961:   Married David Harter, 20 May. Student production of *Easy Death* at the Oxford Playhouse. Student sound production of *You've No Need to be Frightened*.
1962:   *The Ants* broadcast on the BBC Third Programme, 27 November, directed by Michael Bakewell.
1963:   Son, Joe Harter, born on 26 April.
1964:   Son, Paul Harter, born on 5 December.
1967:   *Lovesick* broadcast on the BBC Third Programme, 2 May, directed by John Tydeman.
1968:   *Identical Twins* broadcast on the B.B.C. Third Programme, 21 November, directed by John Tydeman.
1969:   Son, Rick Harter, born on 30 September.
1971:   *Abortive* broadcast on the B.B.C. Third Programme, 4 February, directed by John Tydeman. *Not . . . not . . . not . . . not . . . not enough oxygen* broadcast on the B.B.C. Third Programme, 31 March, directed by John Tydeman.
1972:   *Schreber's Nervous Illness* broadcast on the B.B.C. Third Programme, 25 July, directed by John

9

Tydeman. Lunchtime stage production, King's Head Theatre, London, 5 December 1972. *The Judge's Wife* televised on B.B.C. T.V., 2 October, directed by James Fermin. *Henry's Past* broadcast on the B.B.C. Third Programme, 5 December, directed by John Tydeman. First production of *Owners*, Royal Court Theatre Upstairs, London, 6 December, directed by Nicholas Wright.

1973: *Perfect Happiness* broadcast on the B.B.C. Third Programme, 30 September, directed by John Tydeman. Lunchtime stage production, Soho Poly, London, 10 March 1975, directed by Susanna Capon.

1974–75: Resident dramatist at the Royal Court Theatre, London.

1974: *Turkish Delight*, televised on B.B.C. T.V., 22 April, directed by Herbert Wise.

1975: First production of *Objections to Sex and Violence*, Royal Court Theatre, 2 January, directed by John Tydeman. Sunday night Theatre Upstairs production of *Moving Clocks Go Slow*, 15 June, directed by John Ashford.

1976: *Light Shining in Buckinghamshire* with Joint Stock Theatre Group, directed by Max Stafford-Clark. Opened at the Traverse Theatre, Edinburgh, 7 September, and at the Royal Court Theatre Upstairs, 21 September. *Vinegar Tom* with Monstrous Regiment, directed by Pam Brighton. Opened at the Humberside Theatre, Hull, 12 October, and at the I.C.A., London, 6 December.

1977: First production of *Traps*, Royal Court Theatre Upstairs, 27 January, directed by John Ashford.

1978: Contributed with Michelene Wandor and Bryony Lavery to Monstrous Regiment's cabaret, *Floorshow*, which opened at the Theatre Royal, Stratford East, 18 January. *The After Dinner Joke* televised on B.B.C. T.V., 14 February, directed by Colin Bucksey. *The Legion Hall Bombing* televised on B.B.C. T.V., 22 August, directed by Roland Joffe. (At their request, Caryl Churchill's and Roland Joffe's names were removed from the credits.)

1979: *Cloud Nine* with Joint Stock Theatre Group, directed by Max Stafford-Clark. Opened at Dartington College of Arts, Devon, 14 February, and at the Royal Court Theatre, 29 March. Revival: Royal Court, September 1980, directed by Max Stafford-Clark and Les Waters. American production: Theatre de Lys, New York, 18 May 1981, directed by Tommy Tune.

1980: First production of *Three More Sleepless Nights*, Soho Poly, London, (lunchtime), 9 June, directed by Les Waters. Transferred to the Theatre Upstairs, August 1980.

1982: *Crimes* televised on B.B.C. T.V., 13 April, directed by Stuart Burge. First production of *Top Girls*, Royal Court Theatre, 28 August, directed by Max Stafford-Clark. Transferred to Joseph Papp's Public Theatre, New York, December 1982. Returned to the Royal Court, February 1983.

1983: *Fen* with Joint Stock Theatre Group, directed by Les Waters. Opened at the University of Essex Theatre, Colchester, 20 January, and at the Almeida Theatre, London, 16 February. Transferred to Joseph Papp's Public Theatre, New York, in May, and to the Royal Court Theatre, London, in July.

1984: First production of *Softcops*, Barbican Pit, London, 2 January, directed by Howard Davies. Contributed with Geraldine Pilgrim, Pete Brooks and John Ashford to *Midday Sun*, which opened at the I.C.A., London, 8 May.

1986: *A Mouthful of Birds* with Joint Stock Theatre Group, written by Caryl Churchill and David Lan, choreographed by Ian Spink, directed by Ian Spink and Les Waters. Opened at Birmingham Repertory Theatre, 2 September, and at the Royal Court Theatre, 25 November.

1987: First production of *Serious Money*, Royal Court Theatre, 21 March, directed by Max Stafford-Clark. Transferred to Wyndham's Theatre, London, July 1987, and to Joseph Papp's Public Theatre, New York, November 1987.

1988: Contributed to *Fugue*, *Dance on 4*, choreographed and directed by Ian Spink, televised on Channel 4, 26 June.

For my niece, Anna, in loving memory

Introduction

On 6 December 1972 *Owners* opened at the Royal Court Theatre Upstairs in London. It was not the first performance of a play by Caryl Churchill. There were a number of student productions of her work while she was at Oxford, and, during the sixties and early seventies, eight of the radio plays were broadcast on the B.B.C. Third Programme. *Owners* was, however, a watershed in her career in that it was the first stage play to receive a professional production. Churchill has maintained the association with The Royal Court that *Owners* initiated. In 1974 she became Writer in Residence there, and the majority of her stage plays have been performed either in the main theatre or the Theatre Upstairs. She has also worked closely with the Joint Stock Theatre Group, and, largely through this connection, with the two major directors of her later work, Max Stafford-Clark, one of the founder members of Joint Stock, and Les Waters.

The Joint Stock work method is based on a close collaboration between actors, writer and director. The normal practice has been to begin with a workshop period, in the course of which the group collectively researches a topic, followed by a writing gap, and then by rehearsals. It is not a way of working with which all writers feel at ease, but Churchill has responded enthusiastically to the sharing of ideas that it entails. Working closely with actors and directors on an approach to performance which encourages innovation and flexibility has facilitated the daring experimentation with structure that is a notable feature of her plays. The communal exploration of a topic, which precedes the writing of a Joint Stock play, has enabled her to develop one of the major themes of her work: the link between personal, inner experience and the larger world of public events.

This interest is strongly evident in Churchill's first play for Joint Stock, *Light Shining in Buckinghamshire*, which takes as its subject matter the abortive hopes for a more egalitarian social order that inspired many radical sects in mid-seventeenth century England. *Light Shining*'s linear structure, taken in conjunction with its juxtaposition of characters and language styles, and its presentation of individual aspirations and their curtailment as integrally connected to a wider quest for transformation, gives the play a richness of texture and thematic clarity that makes it a valuable introduction to Churchill's work. For this reason, and because of its key position as her first Joint Stock play, I have devoted Chapter One to a detailed exploration of it.

The second chapter opens with a discussion of *Vinegar Tom* which was written for the feminist theatre group Monstrous Regiment in the same year as *Light Shining in Buckinghamshire*, and shares with it a common historical background. The remainder of Chapter Two focuses on Churchill's other work to date for the Joint Stock Theatre Group: *Cloud Nine*, *Fen* and *A Mouthful of Birds*. Chapter Three examines seven of the radio plays, beginning with *You've No Need to be Frightened* which had a student production in 1961. Chapters Four and Five discuss, in varying ways, Churchill's recurrent fascination with the forces working towards, and against, change in individuals and society. The five plays which are considered in Chapter Four have all been performed at the Royal Court, and range from *Moving Clocks Go Slow*, which was given a Sunday night Theatre Upstairs production in 1975, to the highly successful *Serious Money*, which transferred from the Court to Wyndhams Theatre, in London's West End, in July 1987. Chapter Five deals with the television plays; a further radio play, *Perfect Happiness*; and two stage plays, *Objections to Sex and Violence* (the first of Churchill's plays to be performed on the main stage of the Royal Court Theatre, in 1975), and *Softcops*, which was premiered at the Barbican Pit in 1984. The conclusion reviews the plays within a chronological context, and comments finally on *Light Shining in Buckinghamshire*.

The route that I have taken through Churchill's plays is therefore a somewhat circuitous one. The advantage of this, hopefully, is that it stresses their interrelatedness whilst avoiding the suggestion that the radio and early stage plays were simply stepping stones towards the later, more mature, works. A flexible approach also seems an apposite response to a playwright one of whose central concerns is the fluid nature of time.

1

Light Shining in Buckinghamshire

The Work Process

Caryl Churchill's first play for the Joint Stock Theatre Group was originally going to be about the Crusades. Max Stafford-Clark had visited a house where there was a crusader's tomb and this had led him to speculate on 'what would make someone uproot himself and set off for Jerusalem.'[1] He invited Caryl Churchill and Colin Bennett to co-write a play on this topic, and the three of them met frequently to discuss ideas and reading. In the course of the discussion period their focus of interest shifted from the Crusades to the seventeenth century. They kept the idea of 'the millennial dream and Max's question of why you would turn your life upside down for it'[2] but, in place of the remote figures of the crusaders whom they'd never been able to imagine very clearly, they 'could hear vivid voices: "Give give give up, give up your houses, horses, goods, gold . . . have all things common."'[3]

The 1640s in England were a time of unprecedented change. The overthrowing of the power of the King was part of a questioning of all forms of authority, and, for a brief but heady time, as huge numbers of ordinary men and women attempted to alter the direction of their lives, a radical restructuring of society seemed possible. In the course of a three-week work-shop in May 1976, the two writers, Max Stafford-Clark and a group of actors worked through improvisation, reading and discussion to develop their understanding of the period and their individual and collective responses to it. As a basis for the work, Churchill devised:

19

> a character for each actor with a speech from before the war, a
> summary of what happened to them and what their attitude
> should be at an improvised prayer meeting, and how they ended
> up at the restoration.[4]

This 'before-during-after idea' became a major structuring
device of the eventual play.

During the nine-week writing period which followed the
workshop Colin Bennett left the project and Caryl Churchill
became the sole writer. The workshop had been an enormously
productive and stimulating experience, and she was overwhelmed with ideas. Her notebooks for *Light Shining* (unpublished) teem with suggestions for scenes and structures.
Characters are developed and then abandoned as new possibilities emerge. Two brief quotations from the notebooks encapsu-
late the mood and format which she gradually discovered.
Around 16th June, there is a diagram:

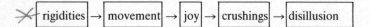

Then, on 30th June, the words: 'like small chips of film, black
and white stills, grainy'. The progression from rigidity, through
movement to joy, then to the crushing of possibilities and a final
state of disillusion is an amplification of the 'before-during-
after' shape. *Lighting Shining* begins with characters imprisoned within tightly confining ideologies and economic and
social structures, and shows their elation and amazed excitement as these 'rigidities' are challenged and loosened. As the
characters take control of their lives the forward momentum of
the play leads to an upsurgence of joy, which is then arrested
and destroyed. Moments of movement and happiness are
found, however, even as hopes diminish, and a mood of ecstatic
fervour precedes the final statement of disillusion.

If this progression defines the play's narrative shape, the
words: 'like small chips of film, black and white stills, grainy',
evoke its texture. Each character and episode has the clarity of
a snapshot, a brief moment of time arrested: each separate

incident has its own meaning and resonance. The 'grainy' quality comes from the cross-referencing of images, ideas and action from one scene to another. The 'before-during-after' shape is created not as an unbroken line, but as a montage of related fragments.

When rehearsals began, the play was still not quite complete. There were six actors and six main storylines and the intention was that, as well as playing his or her own character, each actor would play minor parts in the other stories. Then the writer and director realized that it might not be necessary to write the missing scenes: 'if it wasn't quite clear which character was which and different actors played the same character in different scenes'.[5] It is an interesting example of the way in which an idea, generated partly by necessity, relates integrally to the play. When the characters are played by a variety of actors, the focus is not on individual lines of narrative, but, instead 'each scene can be taken as a separate event rather than part of a story.'[6] In this way an accretion of small, but detailed fragments of various lives all linked by shared hopes is created. All the separate incidents come together in the huge event of the attempted revolution.

The Play

Rigidities

Light Shining in Buckinghamshire opens with the singing of verses from Isaiah, which describe a time of terror and cataclysmic upheaval. The earth is shaken to its foundations, but escape is impossible. The 'pit' and the 'snare' lie waiting, and whoever avoids one falls into the other. The first image is expressive of both turmoil and lack of freedom: it creates a backdrop of momentous happenings in front of which human beings are depicted in petrified attitudes of terror. Out of this sense of universal nightmare three subsequent images coalesce, of characters frozen within rigidly confining structures.

The first scene is a monologue. Cobbe (who is loosely based on an actual person, a Ranter named Abiezer Coppe or Cobbe) prays for reassurance that he is one of God's elect, the privileged few who in the next life will be saved from the terrors of hell. He is a gentleman, and so is a member of the minority group who enjoy the good things of this world. Cobbe prays for forgiveness for his sins, but is overcome by a compulsion to use Christ's name blasphemously. He longs to overthrow the authority of God the father, and also of his earthly father.

> At table last night when father said grace I wanted to seize the table and turn it over so the white cloth slid, silver, glass, capon, claret, comfits overturned. I wanted to shout your name and damn my family and myself eating so quietly when what is going on outside our gate?

Cobbe yearns to break out of the straitjacket of his background and beliefs, but is afraid to do so. He is caught in the bind that not to honour his father is a sin, but at the same time he feels deeply that it is sinful to honour someone so 'greedy, cruel' and 'hypocritical'. It is as sinful to remain where he is and not to go down to his father before he leaves the house as it is to go to him. At the end of the scene he makes the decision to stay where he is, and so avoid his father's blessing. Within the rigidity depicted by the first scene there is, therefore, some loosening of bonds. Cobbe's refusal to go to his father is a mental shift, involving a rejection of parental authority.

In the first scene the effect of authority figures is felt, but not seen. In the following two scenes representatives of authority are shown alongside victims of the system. Cobbe is a gentleman, but Claxton in scene two, and Brotherton in scene three, are trapped at the bottom of a rigid hierarchical structure. In scene two an Anglican vicar talks to his servant about the reasons for the current fighting:

> Why we have this war is because men want heaven now. If God meant us to have heaven on earth, why did he throw us out of paradise?

He situates heaven firmly in the afterlife. As far at least as the poor are concerned, this earthly life is meant to be one of

tribulation and suffering. ' "Be afflicted and mourn and weep."
That is the way to heaven.' As an agent of the governing élite,
he, however, is exempt from a state of constant privation. As he
talks of the necessity that the poor should submit to the will of
God and his representatives on earth, he drinks wine and eats
oranges.

The servant's name is not spoken in the dialogue and is given
in the text only in brackets. Like Cobbe, the character of
Claxton is based on an actual historical figure (Laurence
Clarkson or Claxton). In this scene he speaks only twelve
words, seven of which are 'sir'. He is a nameless functionary,
defined only by his servant status. The reality and hardship of
his life are glimpsed only through the occasional questions
which the Vicar deigns to ask him about a sick child. The
employer focuses on his servant's problems for long enough to
make him a present of an orange for the baby, then tells him
that if the child dies he must submit. 'We all have to suffer in this
life.' To help wash down this unpalatable thought, he has
another drink of wine.

In the third scene there are two authority figures, and one
victim. Margaret Brotherton, who is on trial for vagrancy, is
caught helplessly whichever way she turns for a way out of her
poverty. She has neither home nor food. If she steals food, she
is liable to be hanged; if she begs, she will be whipped; if she
does neither she will starve. At a time of increasing enclosure of
the common land, large numbers of men and women were
being made homeless. They had no place within the current
economic structure and harsh laws deprived them of any rights
except those of starvation and helplessness. Margaret Brotherton has no means of livelihood. She is unmarried, and, in a
society based on property, has not even the small degree of
protection that would be awarded to her as a man's possession.
She scarcely understands the questions the two justices of the
peace put to her. The few times she does reply her answers
are 'barely audible'. She is found guilty of vagrancy and
sentenced:

> to be stripped to the waist and beaten to the bounds of [the] parish
> and returned parish by parish to . . . the parish where [she was]
> born.

Margaret Brotherton is just one in a list of defendants. At the beginning of the scene the J.P.s discuss the previous case, and, at the end, they call for the next defendant. Both she and Claxton are almost silent. Articulacy is the prerogative of those in authority. Claxton and Brotherton seem not so much individuals as representatives of many, unknown, suffering men and women. Cobbe is articulate, but he constantly strives to bite back the blasphemous words that he really wants to utter. Blasphemy would be an act of rebellion, an overturning of everything his society holds sacred. All three characters are seemingly trapped within their circumstances like flies in amber.

Movement

The following scenes show the first stirrings of movement. At a prayer meeting, Star, a corn merchant, recruits for the parliamentary cause. Under the rule of the King, he tells the congregation, they live the life of slaves but the Kingdom of Jerusalem is at hand. Very soon, in only a few years time, Christ will come to earth and establish Jerusalem, heaven on earth. If they join the army to defeat Antichrist, which is the King, they will be Christ's saints and they 'will rule with Jesus a thousand years.' At the end of the scene one of the listeners, Thomas Briggs, gives his name as a soldier.

The subsequent scene, 'Brotherton Meets the Man', picks up on the notion of the imminence of Christ's coming. In the course of her wanderings, Brotherton meets an unnamed man: in a cold, windy and desolate place the two of them discuss their few possessions. Brotherton learns that the man has tenpence, and offers to sell him a rope and a piece of cloth for a halfpenny. Instead, the man bargains with her that he will give her the money if she will first lie down with him: 'Out of the wind.' With tenpence, Brotherton tells him, they can get indoors. The money would 'Last more than one day', and 'Even one day's good.' The man would feel better if he knew how soon Christ was coming.

MAN: If only the money would last till the world ends then it would be all right. It's warm in heaven.

BROTHERTON: If he comes tomorrow and you've not drunk your money. Sitting here with tenpence in the cold. Christ laugh at you for that.

Despite the bleakness of the setting and the poverty of the characters, there is some sense of liberation. Brotherton is on the road, free from persecution, if only temporarily. The man is able to foresee a better time when Christ's kingdom will be established on earth. Brotherton rejects the values of thrift and care for the morrow. This, too, is a kind of bondage, and in her negation of it Brotherton focuses attention away from paradise in the afterlife, and comfort and good things tomorrow, to the present moment and the possibility of happiness now.

The next two scenes show first Briggs and then, to a greater extent, a new character – Jone Hoskins – taking over control of their lives. In 'Briggs Joins Up' Briggs asserts his independence by keeping his hat on in Star's presence and declining to call him 'sir'. Star explains to Briggs more fully, the reasons for the fighting:

You're a Saxon. I'm a Saxon. Our fathers were conquered six hundred years ago by William the Norman. His colonels are our lords. His cavalry are our knights. His common foot soldiers are our squires. When you join this army you are fighting a foreign enemy. You are fighting an invasion of your own soil. Parliament is Saxon. The Army is Saxon. Jesus Christ is Saxon. The Royalists are Normans and the Normans are Antichrist. We are fighting to be free men and own our own land.

What Star effectively does is to give Briggs a history, and so a sense of identity. It is the rulers and conquerors whose stories are known; the poor are largely without a recorded history. *Light Shining* depicts men and women in the process of self-definition.

If the poor form the base of the hierarchical structure, women are at the very bottom of the heap. Churchill shows women caught not only in the trap of poverty, but also of traditional, male-imposed views of their uncleanliness and essential wickedness. At a number of points in the play women

25

are seen to be rigidly confined not only by their poverty but also by their lack of self-worth. When Jone Hoskins disrupts a religious service in scene six, she speaks out against the view that only men should have the right to preach and to interpret the Bible. Briggs gains a sense of personal and class history through an identification with the Saxon cause; Hoskins asserts her right to preach, and to offer men and women the message that they are of value in themselves. The Calvinist preacher tries to impose a new hierarchy, in which only an elected few will get to heaven, in place of earthly privilege. 'Look into your hearts and see whether God has chosen you', he tells his congregation. Hoskins counters him with the words: 'He's chosen me. He's chosen everyone.'

The forward movement from the rigidity of the first scenes is not unhindered; there are counter pressures that hold back the forward impetus. The preacher has Hoskins ejected from the service and, in the following scene, Claxton's wife is unable to accept Hoskins's view of the role of women:

> . . . women can't preach. We bear children in pain, that's why. And they die. For our sin, Eve's sin. That's why we have pain. We're not clean.

Even in the scene 'Briggs Joins Up', there is a suggestion of the limitations to freedom of thought which will be accepted in the Parliamentary army. Star asks Briggs at the end of the scene if he will obey orders. 'If they're not against God', he replies. 'They can't be against God', says Star, 'in God's army.'

At this point in the play, however, the impulse towards self-realisation gathers momentum as characters are shown seizing the moment and taking control of their lives. 'Claxton Brings Hoskins Home', 'Cobbe's Vision', 'Two Women Look in a Mirror', and 'Briggs Recalls a Battle' all contain visions of a new kind of society and sense of self. 'Claxton Brings Hoskins Home', shows Claxton in the process of seeing the society he lives in as the alienating place it is, and finding in a biblical text the motive power to express his sense of dispossession.

> 'And I saw a new heaven and a new earth; for the first heaven and the first earth were passed away. And there was no more sea.'

'Why no more sea?' he asks, and gives his own answer in a wonderful and disturbing image of the sea as a bitter element in which the rich and their agents – the squire, parson, 'Bailiff, Justices, Hangman' – swim like fish, but in which the poor drown. He is 'a drowned man', but in the new heaven and earth he will be able to breathe because there will be 'no more sea'.

Joy

The words in the following scene are taken from *A Fiery Flying Roll* by Abiezer Coppe. This historical material gives an added dimension and authority to Claxton's vision. Cobbe describes a time of personal desolation and then, in highly individual and ecstatic language, the experience that rescued him from this. His central vision is of God not as an external, regulating force, but as an inner means of self-affirmation and realization: God within individual men and women.

This affirmation is beautifully physicalized in the next scene. One woman sits mending, another enters with a piece of broken mirror. She has brought it from the big house which, in the owner's absence, she went into with a group of local people. They burned the Norman papers that were the owner's deeds to the land, but not the corn because it's their corn now. Everyone took something from the house, but there was so much that she didn't know what to choose. As the two women look in the fragment of mirror, she describes a huge mirror in the house where it is possible to see the whole of one's self at once. 'They must know what they look like all the time. And now we do.' To see oneself in a mirror is to gain both a certain objectivity and a sense of indentity. In the mirror, the woman sees reflected a new self and a vision of a new kind of society.

Claxton, Cobbe, and the women learn new ways of seeing: Briggs's vision is one of community and brotherhood. In the midst of the horrors of battle he realizes that the soldiers are not fighting each other but Antichrist, and that even the soldiers on the other side would be made free and glad when they saw the 'paradise' that had been won. 'Darkness and confusion' give way to 'quiet and sunlight', 'pain' to 'joy'.

Briggs's speech leads into the singing of eight lines from *Song of the Open Road* by Walt Whitman. It is the high point of hope in the play, and the greatest upsurgence of joy. Everything seems possible in this song of the inherent beauty of all things, and the free and reckless giving of self.

The long scene which ends the first half of the play is a cut-down version of the Putney Debates of October and November 1647. The Army Council meet to consider proposals put forward by the Levellers in the form of an Agreement of the People. Rainborough, Wildman and Sexby argue that all men should have some share in the choosing of those who make laws under which everyone must live. Cromwell and Ireton argue in favour of the rights of property. With the exception of this final one, all the scenes in the first act are brief. One 'still' follows another in rapid succession, as rigidities dissolve and a vision of a new heaven and earth seems briefly to be an achievable reality. The lengthy debate which concludes the act curtails this possibility. The restructuring of society which follows the defeat of the King will be a relatively minor one. Those who have always been at the bottom of the heap will once again be imprisoned there.

The second half of the play shows the further destruction of hope and joy. The Army puts down an attempt by the Diggers to set up a more justly based society at St. George's Hill in Surrey through the collective cultivation of the common land, and brutally suppresses a Leveller uprising. As Star warns Briggs:

> If everyone says and does what he likes, what army is it? What discipline is there? In army or government. There must be some obedience. With consent, I would say, yes, but then you must consent, or – what? If every man is his own commander?

After the war Star takes over the property and authority of the old squire. He tells the Vicar who welcomes him that he doesn't want to treat his tenants harshly, but it will, however, be necessary to enclose the common land.

I don't mean in the old sense, as the old squire did. I mean to grow corn. To make efficient use of the land. To bring down the price of corn. I'm sure the tenants will understand when I explain it to them.

The scene which follows furthers the re-establishment of the rigid constraints of poverty and hopelessness. Unable to make milk to feed her baby, a half-starved woman plans to leave her outside the mayor's house in the hope that she will be taken care of. Now that the moment has come she is unable to put the baby down. 'You're not doing it for you', a woman friend tells her. 'It's for her . . . Don't talk. Do it. Do it.' 'If she was still inside me', is the hopeless rejoinder. The only way the woman could protect her child would be if she could somehow take her back inside her body.

'A Woman Leaves her Baby' is followed by the monologue, 'A Butcher Talks to his Customers'. The customers are by implication the audience and, in language characterized by a staccato rhythm and relentless, biting anger, the Butcher berates them for their greed: 'Was yesterday's veal good?' It couldn't have been, or they wouldn't 'want a capon today'. 'You don't look hungry', he tells an imaginary customer.

You look less like a man needing a dinner than anyone I've ever seen. What do you need it for? . . . To stuff yourself, that's what for. To make fat. And shit. When it could put a little good flesh on children's bones.

The suffering of children is a dark thread woven into the play. In scene two the motif of the dying child is introduced, then picked up in scenes four and seven. In 'A Woman Leaves her Baby', the only scene in which a baby is actually represented on stage, the child is the central focus of the scene and the subject of all the spare, haunting dialogue. The placing of this scene between 'The Vicar Welcomes the New Landlord' and 'A Butcher Talks to his Customers' creates a complex set of resonances. By implication the women are starving because of the forced enclosure of the common land. In place of the promised New Jerusalem, they find themselves in a hellish

29

landscape of privation and despair. The directness of the Butcher's address brings the image of the starving child up to date and implicates the audience in the guilt of the property owners.

> You've had their meat that can't buy any meat. You've stolen their meat . . . You cram yourselves with their children's meat. You cram yourselves with their dead children.

The Butcher's speech therefore opens the action of the play outwards, extending it into the present day, and the hungry two thirds of the world's population that underlie the relative affluence of the rest. The scale of the event of the failed revolution is increased also by the earlier inclusion of discussion of the action of the parliamentary forces in Ireland. Briggs rejects Star's view of the Irish as traitors. To him, they are fighting for freedom and liberty, exactly as he once believed that the Army was doing in England. 'If I was Irish I'd be your enemy', he tells Star. 'And I am.'

Following the suppression of the Levellers and the Diggers, many men and women sought fulfilment of their awakened hopes in the beliefs of ecstatic sects like the Ranters. The second scene of Act Two is a monologue in which Claxton, now known as the Captain of the Rant, describes how he came to realise that there is no such thing as sin. In order to be free of the imprisoning belief in sin, it is necessary to: 'commit it purely, as if it were no sin'. Mentally and physically he is still moving forward: he has left everything he knows behind him, and feels himself impelled to rush ever more quickly onwards, 'towards the infinite nothing that is God.'

The long final scene of the play is a meeting of the Ranters. Five of the characters have appeared in previous scenes; one, the Drunk, is new. Hoskins still sees the present as a magical time when human beings are transformed by the imminence of Christ's coming:

> . . . you see men and women shining now, everything sparkles because God's not far above us like he used to be when preachers stood in the way, he's started some great happening and we're in it now.

30

Hoskins, Claxton and Cobbe in their various ways have a vision of the immanence of God within human beings and the natural world. Cobbe sees the presence of God in the poorest and most degraded of men. Claxton realises that:

> . . . there's no God or devil outside what's in creation. But in us. I know we can be perfect.

This perfection will be achieved through the rejection of property. All things must be held in common: goods – and bodies too. My husband or wife: 'that's property'.

In 'The Meeting' the characters create a new form of communion service. Hoskins holds out an apple: 'It comes to me God's in it. If a man could be so perfect.' From the perfection of the apple they look to the latency of this in human beings. Three of the characters are separated from the rest. The Drunk sits apart. Briggs is isolated by his loss of Faith. He no longer believes that Christ will come: everything he's learned has been for nothing. Brotherton is imprisoned by her sense of guilt. No-one must touch her, she tells them. She killed her baby: 'The same day it was born.'

Her admission carries the child motif, with its linked references to suffering and guilt, through to the climactic moment of the play. The baby's death is not her sin, Briggs tells her, but 'one more of theirs. Damn them.' Claxton reassures her as to her essential goodness, God is present within her, she is 'lovely . . . perfect'. As Brotherton gradually allows herself to be touched, she becomes both the centre and the physical representative of the communion between them all. Their joint action is sacramental in that it is the outward and visible sign of their belief in their own worth, and in the resultant multitude of possibilities which exist for movement and change.

> Everything's moving. God's going right through everything . . .
> Everything new, everything for the first time, everything starting –

After the crushing of the Levellers and the Diggers, this communion service of the Ranters presents a final and estatic vision of an overturned world. God is present within them all, sanctifying and transforming the present moment. 'Yes, yes, God's here, look, God now –' The scene ends with the singing of verses from Ecclesiastes which affirm a justice greater than that of men, and the right of all to share in the good things of the earth.

Disillusion

The meeting of the Ranters is the final glimmer of hope. The epilogue, in which the characters talk about their lives after the Restoration, creates a sense of fragmentation. Briggs has the longest speech. He describes how his wish to eat too little, and so to redress the balance against those who eat too much, led him to force his body to live on grass. The play ends with images of immobility and silence. If anyone comes to watch Briggs, he stands 'stock still' until the visitor goes. Claxton has lost faith in the possibility of perfection. He has emigrated to the Barbados, where occasional news of the world he left behind reaches him. 'I give it the hearing and that's all', he says. 'My great desire is to see and say nothing.'

Light Shining ends with hopes extinguished and all forward movement forcibly arrested. The experience which the play presents for an audience is, however, only partially a bleak one. Though the throughline leads to a state of disillusion, both the positioning of the scene of the Ranters' meeting and the whole structure of the play, which is created through the montage effect of adjacently placed 'black and white stills', leave the audience with a strong sense of the possibility of a major revolution in the way human beings might live together, as well as its suppression. The short, self-contained scenes, Brechtian in this as well as in the precision of their action, create a new way of seeing for the audience as well as the characters. In place of the clear, causal links of a detailed narrative, there is a proliferation of events, each linked to the others through a shared set of hopes and beliefs. The advantage of this method is that the failure to establish a New Jerusalem is in no way shown to be inevitable. The various sects fail not because of personal inadequacy, but because they are crushed from above.

At the beginning of scene six the Calvinist preacher gives as his text for the day, Psalm one hundred and forty nine: 'Sing unto the Lord a new song and his praise in the congregation of saints.' His message is new, however, only in its substitution of one form of aristocracy for another. 'In Christ's kingdom no worldly honour counts. A noble can be damned and a beggar saved', but, 'those that are not saved will be cast into the pit.' Heaven is only for the elect. In contrast, the lines from Whitman's *Song of the Open Road* are a hymn to the joyous realization of self and a carefree giving and sharing with others. From this point on the newly discovered sense of joy is gradually crushed, but the Ranters in the meeting scene achieve a final defiant and ecstatic communion through their rejection of individual ownership of property and affirmation of the intrinsic worth of all human beings. In their philosophy each man and woman is God: all are chosen. This exploration of a discovery of self-worth is one of the elements that links *Light Shining* most strongly to the later Joint Stock plays, and also to the play which Churchill wrote in 1976 for Monstrous Regiment, *Vinegar Tom*.

2

Other Joint Stock Plays and Vinegar Tom

After *Light Shining*, Caryl Churchill's next play to be performed was *Vinegar Tom*, by Monstrous Regiment. There was no workshop period, but the writing overlapped that of *Light Shining* in time and, to a certain extent, in ideas. It seems sensible, therefore, to discuss *Vinegar Tom* before considering the remaining Joint Stock plays.

Like *Light Shining*, *Vinegar Tom* is set in the seventeenth century. The revolutionary possibilities which are the subject of *Light Shining*, as men and women reject old orthodoxies and look into themselves for guidance, are touched on in the first scene: 'There's some in London say there's no sin. Each man has his own religion nearly'. Instead of the precise background of historical events in *Light Shining*, however, Churchill places the action against a broader and more generalized canvas of social upheaval. Her basic concern this time is with the oppression of women. English society in the seventeenth century was in a process of accelerated change from an essentially feudal structure to a capitalist one. The women who are accused of witchcraft in the play are on the margins of society, their real 'crimes' are those of poverty and unorthodoxy (usually of a sexual nature). *Vinegar Tom* is 'a play about witches with no witches in it'.[7] Witchcraft exists only in the minds of the accusers.

Four women are accused of being witches, and are eventually hanged. Joan Noakes is poor, and old. Alice, her daughter, rejects the accepted sexual norms, she has an illegitimate child and sleeps with any man who takes her fancy. In the first scene of the play she has just made love with an unnamed man. His response is to call her a whore. She's not a wife, or a widow, or a

34

virgin: 'whore' is the only category left. Susan is a wife, but she has three small children and has had as many miscarriages. She is pregnant again and terrified because she nearly died giving birth to the youngest child. She takes the abortant, which Ellen, the cunning woman, gives her, but she is consumed with guilt about what she has done. When she is accused of witchcraft, she accepts the fact that she is guilty: 'I was a witch and never knew it . . . I didn't know I was so wicked.' Like Claxton's wife in *Light Shining*, she has learned that the pain of childbirth 'is what's sent to a woman for her sins.' A 'woman tempts man', and 'pays God with her pain having the baby.'

At the end of the play Susan is helplessly trapped by her acceptance of male-imposed ideas of the essential wickedness of women. She believes that she has been a bad mother, and therefore it must also be true that she is a witch. Before she is hanged, Joan Nokes claims to be a witch. Her old cat, Vinegar Tom, she says, is one of her imps. For Joan the idea of herself as a witch is a form of escape from powerlessness. Witches are potent beings who can destroy people who mistreat them. Alice knows that neither her mother nor herself are witches, but, while she waits her turn to be hanged, she expresses the wish that she were.

> If I could live I'd be a witch now after what they've done . . . If I only did have magic, I'd make them feel it.

From the beginning Alice rejects contemporary stereotypes of women; at the end of the play she is vividly and powerfully angry.

Two other women, Betty and Ellen, assert, in different ways, their right to independence. Scene six, in which Betty is tied to a chair to be bled by a doctor, is adapted from a scene that Churchill originally wrote for *Light Shining* as part of Hoskins's early life, but which she was unable to find a place for in the Joint Stock play. Like many of the characters in *Light Shining* and the other women in *Vinegar Tom*, Betty is trapped by her circumstances. She is from a wealthier background than the others, but she has been locked up in her room because she has refused to marry the man her father has chosen for her. When she is bound to the chair, she asks:

> Why am I tied? Tied to be bled. Why am I bled? Because I was screaming. Why was I screaming? Because I'm bad. Why was I bad? Because I was happy.

All the women are constrained by imposed notions of who they are and how they should behave. Betty is literally tied down because she was bad and happy: the two are seen as synonymous. In the second scene, she describes how she climbed a tree, and 'wanted to jump off. And fly.' Instead, she turns her back on the possibility of freedom and agrees to marry the man of her father's choice in order to avoid the danger of being identified as a witch. Flying is one of the traditional activities of witches, a way of escaping from constraints. Betty realises that it would be safer to conform to what is expected of her.

Ellen, the cunning woman, is more clear-sighted than the other women, but she is unable to save herself from the accusation of witchcraft. Packer, the witch-finder, considers cunning women to be the worst witches of all.

> Everyone hates witches who do harm but good witches they go to for help and come into the devil's power without knowing it.

Ellen understands her situation but she is as powerless as the others to do anything about it. She considers the possibility of asking to be swum. A person was pronounced innocent of witchcraft if he or she sank in water instead of floating. It's easy enough to sink. 'Any fool can sink.' Ellen's problem is how to sink without drowning. She is tied even more helplessly than Betty; for her there is no way out.

Vinegar Tom is both simpler and more didactic than *Light Shining*. It presents a clear, linear narrative, punctuated by songs, which forcefully, and sometimes aggressively, point up the present day relevance of the play. Churchill has stated the importance of the songs being sung out of character, by actors in modern dress. Their effect is to extend the frame of reference of the play, and link past oppression and exploitation with their present day manifestations. The gentle, penultimate song, 'Lament for the Witches', asks 'Who are the witches now?'

> Look in the mirror tonight.
> Would they have hanged you then?
> Ask how they're stopping you now.

We are related more closely than we realize to the women who were hanged and burned for trying to assert an independence which their society was unable or unwilling to grant them. 'Who are the witches now? . . . Here we are.'

The final scene of the play is in the form of a music hall double-act, most of the dialogue for which is taken directly from a late medieval handbook on witches by Kramer and Sprenger, *Malleus Maleficarum* (*The Hammer of Witches*). According to the authors of the book, there are more female than male witches because women are more credulous, impressionable and dishonest than men, and they also have feebler intellects. Above all: 'All witchcraft / comes from carnal lust / which is in woman / insatiable.' The final song, 'Evil Women', confronts the men in the audience with their continuing need to see sex, and therefore women, as sinful and dirty. 'Women were wicked to make you burn? . . . Witches were wicked and had to burn.'

Although *Vinegar Tom* is very different in structure and mood from *Light Shining*, Churchill again presents characters who are trapped by externally imposed constraints, and then contrasts this with a loosening of bonds. Betty and Ellen are defeated, but Betty longs for freedom, and Ellen is a strong and independent woman. Alice comes to the point of understanding her own latent power, and is able to articulate her anger at its forced suppression. Most important of all the play's dual perspective is a constant reminder of the possibilities which exist now, as well as those that were denied in the past. *Vinegar Tom*'s real concern is with the legacy we carry with us today from the witches and their accusers. Accusing someone of witchcraft is a way of externalizing all kinds of hidden and unacceptable emotions. Witches are society's scapegoats, and, as such, they are still very much with us.

Cloud Nine

The Work Process

Cloud Nine, Churchill's second play for the Joint Stock Theatre Group, was again directed by Max Stafford-Clark, who was interested, once more, in the theme of people changing their lives, this time with regard to emigration. The original plan was that the first half of the play would be set in Europe and the second in America, with workshops and performances in both England and the States. Arrangements for the American side of the project fell through, however, and Caryl Churchill suggested that she would like to do something instead on sexual politics.

The group of actors who took part in the *Cloud Nine* workshop in the Autumn of 1978 were chosen for their varied sexual backgrounds, as well as for acting ability. In the *Light Shining* workshop the group had explored the material from the outside in, learning about a distant event and then finding out how they related to it. The workshop this time went from the inside outwards. The group began from their own experience and shared details of their personal and sexual lives. They examined sexual stereotypes, and the relationship between gender and status. Max Stafford-Clark devised a status game based on the numbers on playing cards. An actor would draw a card, and, as a result, be assigned a particular level of status from which to respond to the rest of the group. Two was the lowest level, and ten the highest. As the actors became more skilful at differentiating between the various levels, the game became more complex, so that they gradually developed situations where a character's status could be reversed.

The workshop lasted for three weeks, and the writing period for twelve. The first format Churchill explored was based on three generations of a family. The opening scene took place at the grandfather's funeral, where the dead man talked to his wife while the children and grandchildren bickered among themselves. She found this too static, however, and early in November she returned to an idea that had been briefly explored in the workshop: 'the parallel between colonial and sexual oppression'.[8] This led to the setting of the first half of the play in a British colony in Africa at the height of Empire.

The second act proved more problematic. Caryl Churchill wanted this to take place in the present day with its questioning of traditional views of status and of roles based on gender, and felt that she needed a looser structure than that of the first half to reflect this fluidity. At first she wrote a series of monologues, but both she and Max Stafford-Clark were unhappy with this idea. The next version, set in Clive's and Betty's retirement bungalow on the rainy southern coast of England, was not particularly successful either. The breakthrough came when she decided to use 'the children's territory'[9] of a park as the setting. Though only one of the characters in Act Two is a child, the others go through a learning and changing process which in a sense returns them temporarily to the status of children.

The Play

Cloud Nine is divided into two dissimilar units, the first of which is farcical, fast-moving and tightly structured, with clear, boldly-drawn characters. The second half seems at first to be from a different play. It is set in a London park in 1979, approximately a hundred years after act one, but the characters have aged only twenty-five years. The action is more diffuse, moving in a seemingly meandering fashion towards a conclusion which vividly and movingly relates the two halves of the play.

The central controlling agent of Act One is the character of Clive. Scene one takes place on the verandah of his house in Africa. It is right to call it 'his' because from the start he asserts his sense of ownership. 'This is my family', he tells the audience.

> . . . Though far from home
> We serve the Queen wherever we may roam
> I am a father to the natives here,
> And father to my family so dear.

39

He introduces *his* wife, son, daughter and servant to the audience, and Churchill's stage directions on casting neatly and wittily point up both Clive's imposition of his view of what the characters are like, and the possible difficulty he might have in maintaining his idea of them. Betty, Clive's wife, is played by a man, and Joshua, the black servant, by a white actor. Betty tells the audience that she is 'a man's creation'. She has no sense of worth in herself as a woman, but wants to be whatever men want her to be. Joshua's ideal is to be whatever white men want. Clive's young son, Edward, is played by a woman, a fact which aptly sums up his difficulty in living up to the 'manly' image which Clive constantly puts before him. Victoria, the two-year-old daughter, is played by a dummy. She is of so little account that she can be alternately petted like a toy, or tossed aside and totally ignored.

Clive sees the people around him in rigid, two-dimensional terms. Betty is 'delicate and sensitive', and represents: 'The piano. Poetry.' Mrs. Saunders, who comes to stay with them, represents sex. Her 'amazing spirit' causes Clive to be in a permanent state of sexual arousal. Edward is, or should be manly, instead of constantly trying to play with Victoria's doll. Joshua is Clive's 'boy' and 'devoted' to him. Harry Bagley, the visiting explorer, is a 'hothead', but also 'a fine man' who 'will be in history books'.

In the face of hilarious and mounting evidence to the contrary, Clive determinedly holds fast to his idea of the other characters. His own rampant sexual pursuit of Mrs. Saunders in no way disturbs his view of women and marriage. 'Women can be treacherous and evil. They are darker and more dangerous than men', but 'The family protects us from that'. As a mistress, Mrs. Saunders is allowed to be sexually alluring, so long as she is not also sexually demanding, but his wife must be pure and passionless. Clive's discovery that Betty has formed a romantic attachment to Harry Bagley gives him something of a jolt, but he quickly reverts to his old view of her: 'You are not that sort of woman. You are not unfaithful to me, Betty.' He continues on his blinkered way, in his pursuit of Mrs. Saunders, and his determination to perform his duty to the Queen by making all the natives as much like Joshua as possible, while mayhem erupts all round him. Betty declares her love to Harry, Ellen in turn professes love to Betty, while Harry turns his attentions to Edward and Joshua, and offstage the natives are in a state of revolt.

In the middle of threatened chaos, Clive continues resolutely on, seeing only what he wants to see. He never learns what has happened between Harry and Edward or Harry and Joshua. When Joshua, who spies on the others for him, tells him that Ellen 'talks of love' to Betty, he refuses even to countenance such an idea. He finally has to recognize Harry's homosexuality when the latter makes advances to him under the mistaken idea that Clive would welcome his attentions. 'Friendship between men is . . . the noblest form of relationship', Clive confides. 'Women are irrational, demanding, inconsistent, treacherous, lustful, and they smell different from us.' Not surprisingly, Harry gets the wrong idea, and his response renders Clive momentarily speechless for the only time in the play. 'Rivers will be named after you, it's unthinkable', he eventually tells Harry: '. . . this sin can destroy an empire.'

The ideals of family and Empire are sacrosanct. Harry, who despite his unorthodox sexuality, sees a number of things from Clive's perspective, climbs mountains and journeys down rivers: 'For Christmas and England and games and women singing . . . The empire is one big family.' Harry likes to think of Betty sitting at home with Edward on her lap, while he goes off exploring. '. . . you are a star in my sky', he tells her (like Clive he seems to want to own the universe). 'You have been thought of where no white woman has ever been thought of before.' It is, as Betty comments, 'one way of having adventures'.

Clive is determined to prevent anyone from having adventures of which he disapproves, but his world is in danger of collapse from the beginning. Betty and Joshua may for the moment act according to his image of them but their casting makes it clear to the audience that this state of affairs is unlikely to last. One day the two of them might begin to wonder what they are really like. Women and Africa are Clive's twin fears and he talks about them in similar terms. The 'whole continent is [his] enemy', and he is determined to tame it as if it were a wild animal, just as he struggles to subdue the 'dark female lust' which threatens to engulf him.

41

Throughout the act Edward is torn between his real nature and his desire to perform the role Clive has prepared for him. He is made to watch the offstage flogging of rebellious native servants and, though sickened by it, decides that 'They got what they deserved.' Later in the scene his mother appeals to him to put the insolent Joshua in his place, and Edward shows that he has learnt to play the white master: 'You move when I speak to you, boy.' The lesson, however, results in his inability to let his mother touch him. At the end of the act, when Joshua finally rebels and raises his gun to shoot Clive, Edward is the only person who sees, but he makes no attempt to warn his father.

The farcical nature of Act One derives from the divorce between what is actually happening and Clive's determination not to see it. In the middle of a native rebellion he and his family celebrate Christmas. Harry does a conjuring trick with a union jack ('What is it that flies all over the world and is up my sleeve?') while the Empire begins to disintegrate around them. The last scene is also the setting for a traditional festivity. The act ends with a wedding, but Clive's ideal of family life is subverted by the fact that the bride and groom are gay. Clive toasts the happy pair, and wishes them all the blessings of the married state. His total refusal to contemplate Ellen's and Harry's real natures is equalled only by his inability to see what Joshua is doing. 'Dangers are past. Our enemies are killed', he tells his hearers, while his 'boy' prepares to shoot him and his son looks on.

In Act One the family are Clive's property. The action is clear-cut because his view of events structures the act. Insurrection simmers just below the surface, and at the end it is in the open. In the second act the characters have rejected, or are in the process of rejecting, other people's views of them. They have aged only twenty-five years because:

> . . . when the company talked about their childhoods and the attitudes to sex and marriage that they had been given when they were young, everyone felt that they had received very conventional, almost Victorian expectations and that they had made great changes and discoveries in their lifetimes.[10]

Victoria and Edward are now grown-up. Victoria is married to Martin and has a small son, Tommy, who is presumed at times to be just offstage but does not appear. Edward is having an affair with Gerry. Betty has recently left Clive, who appears only briefly towards the end of the act, and is finding life alone a frightening business. The characters are now beginning to make contact with their real selves, and this is underlined by the fact that, with one exception, they are played by actors of the right sex. The exception is Cathy, who is the only child character. She is played by a man in part to balance the fact that Edward was played by a woman:

> partly because the size and presence of a man on stage seemed appropriate to the emotional force of young children, and partly, as with Edward, to show more clearly the issues involved in learning what is considered correct behaviour for a girl.[11]

The first scene takes place in an indoor children's playcentre in a park on a winter's afternoon. The three subsequent scenes are set outside in the park, and the year progresses through spring to a summer's night, and then to an afternoon in late summer.

The characters, particularly those who continue from Act One, are in the midst of attempts to change the direction of their lives, but they find themselves bewildered, and at times alarmed, by the number of choices open to them. Clive is no longer around to tell them what they are like or what to do, and the result is invigorating but also somewhat frightening.

Victoria has been offered a job in Manchester, and is unable to make up her mind whether or not to take it. Martin professes to be sympathetic to her difficulty in understanding what she really wants, but in reality sees the problem only in the way it affects himself. Gerry feels hemmed in by Edward, whom he claims is behaving just like a wife. Edward is nervous of publicly stating his homosexuality in case he loses his job as a gardener in the park. Lin has no such inhibitions about discussing her lesbianism, but she still threatens her daughter with the traditional bogeyman when she's naughty, just as her mother used to frighten her. 'I've changed who I sleep with', she tells

Victoria who accuses her of inconsistency, 'I can't change everything.'

All the characters manage to change at least a little during the act. The park is a kind of playground where they try out different roles and possibilities. Victoria begins a relationship with Lin, and Edward, who has temporarily had enough of men, decides that perhaps he's a lesbian too, and moves in with them. Martin takes turns with the three of them in looking after Lin's child and Tommy. Betty faces the hardest task in trying to change her life because she is older than the others and more set in her ways. Now that she is alone, she often feels very frightened. When she walks in the park, it seems as though she is marooned in the middle of a vast space. It is so large that 'the grass seems to tilt'. She no longer knows who to do things for, and is overcome by the sense that she doesn't really exist. She has never believed that women are of much value, and she finds it almost impossible to believe in her own self-worth.

The rambling attempts of the characters to find new directions for their lives are channelled and given further impetus in scene three. On a hot summer night a drunken Victoria, Lin and Edward attempt, half-jokingly, to conjure up a fertility goddess.

> . . . Lady, give us back what we were, give us the history we haven't had, make us the women we can't be.

History in our culture is largely the stories of the most dominant men: a woman is cut off from her story. Victoria is not able to contact a specifically female history, but her words act as a magnet for wandering spirits. The ghost of Lin's soldier brother, killed in Northern Ireland, enters and his description of the savage boredom of his time in Belfast reveals one aspect of 'the bitter end of colonialism'.[12]

The dead soldier and the living characters exit, and Gerry enters; he, too, conjures up a ghost, by twice calling Edward's name. Edward from Act One appears, and, in words almost identical with an earlier passage between himself and Harry, he and Gerry pledge their love. This is followed by the 'Cloud Nine' song, with its joyous affirmation of sexual possibilities.

The invocation to the goddess leads to the summoning up of ghosts. On the stage, of course, a ghost can be as real as a living character. The past in *Cloud Nine* is presented as solid and tangible, capable of affecting the present. The present moment also contains the possibility of a radical re-orientation of the way we see things, its: 'Upside down when you reach Cloud Nine.'

The suggestion of an overturned world in scene three is not the only echo of *Light Shining in Buckinghamshire*. The constraints that are imposed on the characters in Act One are connected, as in *Light Shining*, with a set of values based on ownership. Betty, Edward and Joshua are Clive's property. Victoria's plea for a history in Act Two is resonant of Briggs's increased understanding of himself and his capacities through his identification with his Saxon past. Betty resembles Brotherton in that she has to fight hard to believe in her worth as a woman. *Cloud Nine* is linked further, both with *Light Shining* and the next two plays Churchill worked on for Joint Stock, through her exploration of time, and, increasingly, of its relationship to the power of theatre. *Light Shining* moves through time in an ordered progression, unlike *Cloud Nine* which dislocates time from one act to another. The Ranters in their meeting focus, however, on the transformative energy that exists in the present moment. They see the latent perfectibility that exists in all natural things. The sacrament of which Brotherton is the centre irradiates a precise moment of time, revealing the fluidity and power that exist within it. Theatre is a focusing of energy within a specific space and time. Churchill's fascination with time in her plays comes partly from an understanding of the power of theatre to use this energy to heighten awareness and to present people at crisis points in their lives when new ways of seeing suddenly open up and change becomes a viable possibility. It stems, too, from an understanding that the present moment is not divorced from the past, or indeed the future; past and future overlap the present and at times all three exist together.

In the final scene of the play all the characters make some progress in their understanding of themselves, and their relationship to others. Betty achieves the most because, from a position of believing that she lacks any intrinsic worth as a

45

woman, she comes to a loving acceptance of herself. Of all the characters she is the one most haunted by her past and fearful of the present moment, but she is able finally to reject Clive's view of her and to embrace the ghost of her past self. The 'Cloud Nine' song is a high point of the play, but the true climax is the loving union of Betty's two identities. Churchill's experiment with time in the play leads to this moment of Betty's acceptance of her former self with all its limitations, and its assimilation into the self she has become. The action of Act Two has progressed against a background of the changing seasons. Scene four is set in late summer, and, for Betty, it is late summer too. Her flowering is especially poignant because it comes in middle age. The final image of the play effects a fruitful and loving relationship between past and present, and opens up the possibility of further transformations in the future.

Fen

The Work Process

The director of the Joint Stock project on *Fen* was Les Waters, who, with Max Stafford-Clark, had co-directed a revival of *Cloud Nine* in 1980, and had also directed a short play by Caryl Churchill called *Three More Sleepless Nights*, which opened at the Soho Poly in June of the same year. There was no change of focus in the pre-workshop phase of *Fen*, as there had been with *Light Shining* and *Cloud Nine*. From the start Caryl Churchill and Les Waters planned to create a piece of theatre based on the Fens. Les Waters has strong family ties with the Fen country, and his commitment to that part of the world was an important factor in the work process from the beginning. He and Caryl Churchill had recently read Mary Chamberlain's *Fenwomen*, with its fascinating details of the day-to-day experiences and memories of women in an isolated Fen village, and this played a part in their decision to concentrate chiefly on the lives of women.

When Churchill began work on the two earlier Joint Stock projects, she had some idea of the ideological premises on which the eventual plays she wrote would be based, even though she didn't at that stage know what form they would take. With *Fen* she felt that she was 'going very openly to see what the place gave'[13] them. The workshop group met in the autumn of 1982 to spend two weeks together in a cottage in the Fens and then a final week in London. In the village the company talked to as many people as possible about their lives. They would go off each day, usually separately, and knock on doors. They asked people about conditions of work, childhood memories, how the village had changed during their lifetimes, and whether they had ever considered moving away from it. Other questions they asked were: What would you like your life to be like? What do you dream of? Later each day, they met up and related the stories they'd heard to each other, and acted out the people to whom they had talked. During the final week in London, they discussed what they'd found out, and what ideas they felt should form part of the play.

We talked about anger and deference – anger and violence, caused by hard conditions of work, turned inward to self-mutilation or deflected on to people who weren't responsible for it. We also talked of women's endurance, and their pride in hard work . . . We wanted to show women constantly working.[14]

The writing gap for *Fen* began in late October and lasted until mid-December. Caryl Churchill's original title for the play was *Strong Girls Always Hoeing*, from a Government Agricultural Report of 1842: 'Strong girls who are always hoeing can do the work better than men and they cost only 1/6 instead of 2/-'. Her *Fen* notebook begins with a list of things that might figure in the play:

picking down the field, candles – letter, lonely woman at door, . . . green mist, old man/woman telling stories, many kinds of housework, suicide, child scaring birds, mutilating animals, baptism, yearning, people of different times in field, evacuees, arson, wanting to retire to 'country', prams round field, woman told lover to murder her, tied cottage, skating, stilts, blind girl, morphrodite . . .[15]

Certain images and ideas recur frequently, informing the search for a unifying structure: the green mist, anger and yearning, gossip, stories, green and pleasant, work, dreams and aspirations. Churchill's first idea for a plot was of 'two women, one who constantly died, and the other who constantly survived',[16] but this didn't fit well with other ideas, and she abandoned it. A couple of weeks into the writing period she began to explore a murder story as the central element, and this became the backbone of the play. Together with the fenland which permeates every aspect of the play, it holds together all the stories and images.

The Play

The opening sequence situates the present day within a historical context of violence and privation. As the audience enter the auditorium, they see a barefoot boy 'from the last century', whose still, fog-shrouded figure appears to have grown out of the earth. He shouts, and waves a wooden rattle to scare away the crows. 'As the day goes on his voice gets weaker till he is hoarse and shouting in a whisper.' It grows dark, and then lighter. Mist still hangs in the air, but the time is now the present. The boy has disappeared and in his place is a Japanese businessman, who welcomes the audience to the 'Most expensive earth in England'. Long ago, he explains, the wild fen people who walked on stilts over the waterlogged ground were known as fen tigers. They resisted the planned drainage of the land by smashing dykes and breaking sluices, but Cromwell, who had previously supported them, realized the advantages of draining the land once he came into power. The result now is: 'Very efficient, flat, land, plough right up to edge, no waste.' Increasingly, the fenland is being sold to business concerns in the City and abroad. The Japanese investor is proud to join the 'many illustrious landowners, Esso, Gallagher, Imperial Tobacco, Equitable Life [who] all love this excellent earth.' He decides, however, to escape from the fog, and find 'teashop, warm fire, old countryman to tell tales.'

The connected narratives in *Fen* create a fluid and seamless interweaving of past and present, waking reality and dreams. The clearest thread which runs through the play is the story of

Val and Frank. Val leaves her husband and children in order to live with Frank, but misses the children so much that she returns to them. Unable to bear life without Frank, she goes back to him, but is haunted by thoughts of her children. The only way out she sees is through death, and she asks Frank to kill her. He refuses, but then, in a moment of desperate anger, murders her. Val is linked to the other women in the play through kinship, work, and the intensity of her longing for an unattainable dream. Her family relationships connect her to the future, through her children, Deb and Shona, and to the past through her mother, May, and her grandmother, Ivy. On her ninetieth birthday, Ivy reanimates moments from her youth: Killing mice at 'Tuppence a score'; the 'quack who said he could cure cancer'; the hundred-year-old man who used to shout, 'Jarvis, Jarvis, come and make my coffin.'

Val, Angela, Shirley and Nell work for the local farmer: picking potatoes, onion-packing, stone-picking. Shirley works constantly, in her home as well as the fields. While Val talks of her hopeless yearning to live both with her children and Frank, Shirley moves from one job to another: 'ironing, mending, preparing dinner, minding a baby.' The baby is one of her grandchildren. She became a grandmother at thirty-two, and, at fifty, believes that she could soon be a great-grandmother. Like Ivy, she recounts anecdotes from the past. As she works and cares for her grandchild, she remembers the still harder life of her girlhood and early married life. There has never been time for her to think or dream.

Unlike Val, most of the characters suppress their longing for a different kind of life. Angela's story is linked with Val's through a child and through her dissatisfaction with her present life. Angela was not born in the Fens, and she finds its landscape and people 'Flat and dull'. Instead of trying to escape into a new life, as Val does, Angela suppresses her angry longing for something different, but it surfaces in her violent mistreatment of her stepdaughter, Becky, whom she tortures, forcing her to stand still for hours and drink scalding hot water. May refers to Val's longing for a life with her lover as a search for the 'Bluebird of happiness'. In May's eyes fulfilment of this kind exists only in fairy stories: in real life it is unattainable. Val discovers that she is right, but when she leaves Frank and returns to her family, she feels slowed-down and disorientated, as though she were surrounded by 'thick nothing'. Most of the characters bury their dreams and aspirations so deep below the surface of their lives that they are rarely conscious of them. Secretly, May has always longed to be a singer, but, when the children ask her to sing for them, she claims to be unable to do so. The children's aspirations for the future are limited. Becky, Deb and Shona sing a song, based on quotations from Mary Chamberlain's *Fenwomen*, about what they want to be when they grow up. Becky longs to be a hairdresser, but even this turns out to be over-ambitious. Instead, she has to join her stepmother working in the fields.

Nell is set apart from the other women by her outspoken criticism of her employers. Some of her fellow workers find her odd and embarrassing. The children are afraid of her and believe that she is 'a morphrodite . . . A man and a woman both at once.' When the children are rude to Nell and try to attack her, she punishes them by imprisoning Shona briefly in a rabbit hutch. 'Are you a witch?' Shona asks her when she is freed, and Nell answers that she is a princess. The witch/princess antithesis expresses in childlike terms Nell's separateness and links with other fairy-tale like elements: Angela, the wicked stepmother; Val's attempt to find the bluebird of happiness; and the fog-enveloped boy at the start of the play, who has a dreamlike, impressionistic quality suggestive of an illustration for a fairy story or a folk tale. Nell is herself a story-teller. As the women pack onions, she entertains them with a long and wonderfully gruesome tale of a seemingly dead body that returned to life. In the dream which ends the play, she crosses the stage on stilts, like a fairy-story-book giant, and describes her rejection of the fen and all it stands for.

The sun spoke to me. It said, 'Turn back, turn back.' I said, 'I won't turn back for you or anyone.'

Underlying every aspect of the characters' lives is the black, fertile earth. The women work on it, even in freezing rain like splinters of ice. Their hard, unremitting toil connects them to previous generations of farm labourers. The frail boy who scared crows at the beginning of the play is succeeded in scene nine by a more potent ghost. Tewson, the local landowner for whom the women work, has just completed negotiations for the sale of his land with a representative from a City firm when he sees the ghost of a woman working in the field. She has toiled there for a hundred and fifty years, and is filled with anger towards Tewson and his ancestors.

> We are starving . . . You bloody farmers could not live if it was not for the poor, tis them that keep you bloody rascals alive, but there will be a slaughter made amongst you very soon. I should very well like to hang you the same as I hanged your beasts.

The Ghost is as real as any of the other women who work in the fields. The past exists alongside the present in the form of stories and memories, and through old acts of injustice. The present day characters repress their anger and dreams, but these first seep into the earth and then rise from it in the semblance of ghosts, and sudden acts of violence. The chief cause of the woman's anger is her baby who 'died starving'. Her words contain echoes of *Light Shining*, and, as in the earlier play, the death of a starving child in the past is linked to present day horrors. 'I live in your house', the ghost tells Tewson. 'I watch television with you. I stand beside your chair and watch the killings.' The Ghost is the funnel through which past and external acts of violence enter the limited world of the fen.

Torn helplessly between her children and her lover, Val is unable to connect with the world around her. Though she finds no fulfilment in life, in death she becomes the means by which previously unexpressed desires are given form. Like the angry ghost, she enables realities beyond the concrete and immediate to find expression. When she is murdered, her ghost cannot be imprisoned within the wardrobe in which Frank places her. He sits with his back to the wardrobe, but she re-enters from the other side of the stage, and all the ghosts and dreams which everyday reality kept at bay enter with her. The intensity of emotion which is always there just below the surface finds expression in waking dreams and haunting tales of past grief

51

and longing. Val becomes a storyteller, first for the dead, and then for the dreaming living.

The end of the play is a summation of all that has gone before, a release from the narrow, confining perspectives which limit the possibility of change in the waking lives of the characters. First, the dead throng around Val. They are invisible to the audience, but she narrates their stories. A ghost herself, she gives form to other ghosts. In her newly dead state, she is conscious of all that lies hidden from the living. One boy in the crowd who press round her died of measles during the First World War. One of the dead '. . . drowned in the river carrying his torch and they saw the light shining up through the water.' They jostle so thickly that it is hard to focus on one story. Val tries to concentrate all her attention on a weak, sickly girl who longs for the coming of spring. When the green mist comes, people throw bread and salt out for the boggarts, who then begin to work to make everything grow again.

Another, stronger image in Val's mind pushes the ailing girl aside. Val does not recognize it, but it is the angry ghost whose baby died starving. The girl returns, still yearning for the green mist that will herald the spring. 'If I could see the spring again I wouldn't ask to live longer than one of the cowslips at the gate.' The next day the green mist comes and the girl becomes well and strong. But a boy picks a cowslip, not even noticing what he is doing, and the girl withers and dies, like the flower.

The ghosts of the past in the second act of *Cloud Nine* disturb the present moment, but out of that disturbance new patterns for the future emerge. In *Cloud Nine* there are only a few ghosts, of the characters' former selves and the remnants of their colonial past. The ghosts that push in on Val from every side are unknown to her. The green-mist-girl is the stuff of folk tales. Boggarts mingle with the human figures in Val's mind so that past and present, the living and the dead mesh together. Val describes a nightmare in which Becky tries to escape from Angela. Becky throws herself at her stepmother in order to wake herself up, but it goes wrong and she finds herself 'falling into another dream' – and entering Val's world. She appears on the stage, followed by Angela, who understands that she hurts Becky in order to prove that she herself exists.

> I stand in a field and I'm not there. I have to make something happen . . . I have to hurt you worse. I think I can feel something. It's my own pain. I must be here if it hurts.

Becky struggles within her dream, refusing to abide by Angela's rules. 'I'm not playing. You're not here', she tells her, and Angela leaves.

Towering on her stilts, like a fen tiger of old, Nell crosses the stage, and Shirley kneels with an iron in her hand, pressing it over the earth, ironing the field. Her endless working in home and on the land have merged. She recalls the stories her grandmother told her, related to her in turn by her grandmother, of how in bad times the people would mutilate the cattle, and her words echo those of the ghost in Tewson's field. The ragged boy who scared crows at the beginning of the play appears, calling: 'Jarvis, Jarvis, come and make my coffin.' He is the hundred-year-old man whom Ivy remembered from her youth. Different moments from many lives, past and present, come together in a single instant of stage time. Then, alongside the other images, is placed that of May who always wanted to be a singer. 'May is there. She sings.'

Past and present and the fantastic world of dreams flow effortlessly into one another at the end of the play. The vivid longing the characters suppress in their waking lives finds expression. May sings, and Nell, huge and free, walks away from the fen. Becky's and Shirley's dreams are violent and painful, but Becky asserts some independence from Angela, and Shirley, in the middle of her hopeless and endless task of ironing the field, makes contact with her younger and more alive self.

> I'd forgotten that. I'd forgotten what it was like to be unhappy. I don't want to.

Though Shirley's memories are unhappy ones, she gains a deeper sense of personal history and a greater consciousness of being alive through reliving them.

At the end of *Cloud Nine* the present day Betty makes loving contact with her earlier self. It is a moment of acceptance and healing. The end of *Fen* is also a healing – of the unreal divorce between waking lives and dreams, and between past and present. Theatre exists only in the present moment, but, within that specific point of time, other times and alternative realities can be created. In *Cloud Nine* Caryl Churchill harnesses the power of theatre to show characters at moments of transformation. In *Fen* Val is the transforming agent by means of which dreams and submerged longings are magically given life.

The Visual Elements of the Production

Before Caryl Churchill began to write *Fen* she had quite a strong sense, from discussion with the company, and particularly with the director and designer, of what it would be like physically. She knew that it would be a continuous piece of theatre, without an interval, that there would be only one set and that any necessary furniture and props would be on stage throughout the performance. Everyone agreed about this. Annie Smart, the designer, also felt strongly that Caryl Churchill should make any demands she wanted in the way of setting and stage effects, and she would then find a way of realizing them. Before the workshop began, Annie Smart was already familiar with the fen landscape: the greys and yellows, and the 'dark pinky-black misty earth',[17] with its seemingly unending vistas receding into the far distance. These elements strongly affected the set she created, but two memories of things she'd seen during the workshop period were particularly powerful sources of inspiration.

The first was a partially demolished house on the edge of the village. One wall was completely gone, and the large garden had become wild. The house had once created a sense of permanence for the people who lived in it, but now the landscape had taken over, 'encroaching into the building itself'.[18] It was an image of transitoriness, and the all-pervasiveness of the fenland. On another occasion she looked through the window of a house in the village, and saw a front room with a fireplace but no carpet, and bales of hay on the floor. It created an extraordinary picture: 'a Magritte feeling. Two worlds collided in a very obvious way.'[19]

The set Annie Smart designed for the production was a

superbly unifying element of the play in performance. It constantly and vividly evoked the power of the fen, and, as in the text, the various aspects of the characters' waking and dreaming lives were shown to be interrelated. It consisted of a furrowed field, surrounded on three sides by the walls of a house. Upstage left was a pile of potatoes, and, a little downstage of this, the large wardrobe in which Frank placed Val's body. The women picked potatoes and stones in the same surroundings in which they lived and worked in their homes, and Val's despairing attempts to find a way out of her dilemma were frustrated always by the fen beneath her feet and the confining walls around her. In scene eleven Shirley set up her ironing board on the field within her house; at the end she ironed the earth itself. When Nell appeared on stilts, it seemed right and logical because escape was possible only by lifting oneself up above the confining walls and floor. At the beginning and end of the performance, mist shrouded the stage, first fog, and then green mist appearing to rise from the fen.

From the opening image through to the final presentation of the dreamworld, the visual element was of great importance. The end of the play had a dancelike quality: movement and gesture were as important as the words, and the physical attitude of each character made a clear and distinct visual statement. Val formed the centre of the stage picture, around whom the other characters created patterns of movement. Some of the characters stood; Shirley knelt as she ironed the field; Frank sat slumped against the wardrobe; Nell briefly filled the stage. Gesture was minimal and precise – Shirley's simple, repeated actions, for example, conjuring up a lifetime of toil. In the next Joint Stock project on which Caryl Churchill worked, movement was an integral part of the structure of the piece from the beginning of the workshop.

A Mouthful of Birds

The Work Process

The work method for *A Mouthful of Birds* (on which Caryl Churchill, Les Waters and Annie Smart worked together again), was a major development in a number of ways. Caryl Churchill and Les Waters wanted to build on the dancelike elements that were present at the end of *Fen*, and the choreographer, Ian Spink, worked with the company from the start, co-directing the production with Les Waters. In addition to the two directors, there were two writers, Caryl Churchill and David Lan, author of *Flight*, *Sergeant Ola and His Followers* and *The Winter Dancers*. Unlike previous Joint Stock projects, there was no writing gap. The whole company worked together for a continuous twelve-week period.

The starting point for the project was *The Bacchae* by Euripides. David Lan, who is an anthropologist as well as a playwright, and whose study of spirit mediums in Zimbabwe, entitled *Guns and Rain*, had been published the previous autumn, was interested in the play from the point of view of possession. Caryl Churchill was particularly interested in the idea of working on 'women and violence, and women being violent, rather than having violence done to them'.[20]

The company worked together throughout the summer of 1986, exploring possession and violence in a present day context. There was never any intention of performing Euripides's play. It was a reference point from which to structure their ideas. They approached the idea of possession in its broadest sense, 'as anything that would make you feel beside yourself, or outside yourself in the normal sense.'[21] They talked to a variety of people: spirit mediums, a transsexual, an anglican vicar who performed exorcisms, and people who'd been in prison for being violent. They were also interested in alcoholism (Dionysos is the god of wine) and in any extreme, other-than-normal state of being.

In daily movement work with Ian Spink, they explored ideas which came up from *The Bacchae* and the interviews. One piece of movement work which developed from *The Bacchae* was connected with fruit:

In *The Bacchae*, women tear up live animals, and [Ian Spink] was exploring fruit as a way of destroying and eating, and tearing something up, which would detach it from pain and guilt . . . and would enable the person doing it to concentrate more sensuously on the pleasures of it.[22]

This work carried over into the production in a movement piece called 'The Fruit Ballet', 'which is all to do with people licking their fingers, the sensuous pleasures of juice, and the terrors of being eaten.'[23] Another dance sequence, 'Extreme Happiness', 'was taken from moments in the actors' lives when they'd been extremely happy' and relates, in the play, 'to the feelings of the women on the mountain.'[24]

From about the middle of the twelve-week period the two writers began to produce scenes for the actors to work on. Creating the play in this way was an exhilarating, but complicated method of working because it was difficult to get a sense of what the overall shape of the piece would be. In the course of two days which the group had spent in the country, living and sleeping in the open, Caryl Churchill had come up with the concept of an 'undefended day'. In the normal course of events we act largely out of habit. The telephone rings, for example, and we answer it. Habit and normality defend us from disturbing ideas and possibilities. If these defences were to break down, the subsequent 'undefended day' would release all kinds of internal and external forces which are normally held at bay. From this came the idea of constructing a piece of theatre which would begin with a group of people living a normal defended day, into which would 'erupt something like the Dionysiac force. You would then get an undefended day, in which people could totally change.'[25]

The Play

Structurally, *A Mouthful of Birds* consists of seven separate stories. The characters are seen first in the course of their normal defended days, there is then a short sequence in which they present excuses for not fulfilling their various engagements. Most of the play consists of the seven stories of possession, between which are enacted fragments from *The Bacchae* story, partly in dance, partly in words. There are also dances expressive of the ecstatic feelings of the characters as they enter into states of possession. All the characters change in the course of the play. At the end there are seven brief monologues in which they talk about what eventually happens to them.

The 'undefended day' is a time of extreme possibilities, in

which the characters are open to possession by their own demons and capacities for ecstasy, and also by external powers. *The Bacchae* story, which invades the action, is a pre-existing set of events, whose horrifying and ecstatic nature provides a central focus for the characters' individual stories of possession. In the first of the seven narratives, 'Psychic Attack', Lena is possessed by a spirit who tells her to murder her baby in order to get rid of the voices in her head. She drowns the child, but the voices continue. Before the start of the next narrative, 'Baron Sunday', there are two acts of possession and a dance sequence. First Dionysos appears to Doreen, who then becomes possessed by Agave and describes the act of tearing up and destroying.

> I put my foot against its side and tore out its shoulder. I broke open its ribs.

This is followed by 'The Fruit Ballet', with its mingled sensuousness and terror, and, then, by Derek's possession by Pentheus, and his description of being torn apart. After Lena's killing of the child, first the perpetrator, then the victim of a past horrific murder speak of that death. 'The Fruit Ballet' includes all the characters in both the terror and the pleasure of the killing.

The play begins and ends with Dionysos dancing. He wears a white petticoat, suggestive of his ambivalent sexuality. At times Dionysos is danced by two performers. He is a double-spirit, an enabler of transformation and ecstasy. Before the last of the seven narratives, Dionysos One and Dionysos Two dress Derek/Pentheus in their female clothes. The climax of the play is the ritual murder of Pentheus, dressed as a woman, by Agave and her Bacchants, while the dual god looks on.

Increasingly, the characters are overwhelmed by irrational, ecstatic forces. Each of them is in a state of transformation, and this releases forces which are both creative and destructive. Doreen becomes so powerful that she can make objects fly across the room. In the 'undefended day' nothing is fixed and static. Derek's possession by Pentheus and his murder are a kind of metaphoric enactment of the changes that occur to him. He begins as an unemployed man who reinforces his sense of maleness by doing weightlifting. In his undefended state he encounters Herculine Barbin, who is played by a woman and is based on a real-life, nineteenth-century, French hermaphrodite. In the course of a lengthy speech about her life, she gives Derek various objects related to her past: a rose, a comb, a crucifix, a lace shawl, a petticoat. At the end of the speech Derek dresses himself in her shawl and petticoat. He sits on the chair where Herculine sat, and 'becomes' her, repeating her speech, and allowing her to take back the objects and pack them away. At the end of the speech, Herculine starts to leave, but, when Derek calls her, she 'turns back and kisses him on the neck'. In performance, the scene is immensely moving. At first when Derek begins the speech for the second time, this seems odd and unnecessary, but, gradually, the recreation of the words by a man opens up all kinds of new possibilities, as well as containing echoes from the first time they are spoken. The repeated lines of dialogue, plus the presence of the man and woman, each dressed in the clothes of the other's sexuality, creates, on stage, a kind of microcosm of the undefended day.

Fluidity of gender is linked to the breaking of other existing moulds, and the possibility of many kinds of transformation. The moment when the standing figure of Herculine kisses the seated man on the neck is erotically tender. It is also reminiscent of the embrace of Betty's two selves in *Cloud Nine*, in being an evocation both of the acceptance of self, and the release of possibilities. Derek's death as Pentheus is the means of his resurrection in a new form, a shamanistic dismembering after which he can be reconstituted differently. At the end of the play he is a woman, joyously at ease in his new body: 'My skin used to wrap me up, now it lets the world in.'

All the characters change during the course of the play, though some more than others. At the end of the play Doreen is possessed by terrifying images of destruction. Her mouth 'is full of birds', whose 'blood and broken bones' threaten to choke her. From the early discussion period Churchill had been strongly interested in women's potential for violence. Women have traditionally been viewed as the peaceful sex, men have fought wars while women stayed quietly at home. All human beings have the potential both for violence and peacefulness, however, and she felt that it was important that women should recognize their own capacity for violence, in order that men could also explore theirs for peacefulness. Part of this process:

> towards being properly peaceful seemed to involve knowing what your power was, but choosing not to use it. For women, it means not being the weak little woman type, but taking on the knowledge of one's own capacity for violence. Then, if one stands for peace, it's from a position of strength and knowledge.[26]

At an early stage in the work process, Caryl Churchill and David Lan discussed a line of development based on this idea. Originally, they planned to begin with 'passive, weak, peaceful women and rather angry, violent men.' The possession stories in the middle section would depict violent women and 'men who are weakened or sexually more uncertain'.[27] This linked with their interest in transsexuality. In communities where possession is a relatively common phenomenon it is frequently people who have very little power or who are on the edge of society who become possessed. This tends to mean either women or men whose sexuality is different from the norms of the society. At the end of the play there would be strong women, 'strong in choosing not to be violent – and more peaceable, unmacho men.'[28]

The idea turned out to be too schematic and, as the writing developed, they didn't try to stick too closely to it. Some of the storylines do follow it through, however. Derek begins by trying to bolster up his idea of himself as a man. He survives a traumatic assault on his sense of self, and finds a truer identity with which he is far more 'comfortable'. 'Was I this all the time? I've almost forgotten the man who possessed this body.'

The original line of development is probably clearest in the character of Lena. At the beginning of the play Lena is too squeamish to skin a rabbit, and her husband does it for her. In the middle section she murders her child, but at the end of the play she understands her capacities, both for caring and destruction. She remembers the pleasure that destruction gave her.

> It's nice to make someone alive and it's nice to make someone dead. Either way. That power is what I like best in the world. The struggle is every day not to use it.

The changes which the characters make in the course of the play are not naturalistic, or particularly logical. The 'unde-fended day' is a sudden, dislocating experience which jolts them into a new dimension, and the possibilities that exist there are nonrational, magic ones. This focus on the stage as a place of magic possibilities is one of the elements which links *A Mouthful of Birds* with the earlier plays. Any discussion of this play in the context of Caryl Churchill's work is complicated by the fact that she co-wrote it with David Lan, and by the integral role which movement plays in the piece. In all her work for Joint Stock she has gained an enormous amount from the collective work method, but, in the case of *A Mouthful of Birds*, there was a cross-fertilization of ideas at every stage.

Some elements in the play do, however, clearly link with Churchill's earlier work. In *Cloud Nine* and *Fen* the stage becomes at times a magic place. The spirits who assault the characters in *A Mouthful of Birds* bear some kinship with the ghosts in the two earlier works. The 'undefended day' is a stepping-aside from everyday reality, a means of releasing alternative realities. Val's murder in *Fen* creates an undiffer-entiated state in which past and present, dreaming and waking all have equal validity. The disruption of normality in *A Mouthful of Birds* frees spirits and demons, along with hidden needs and desires. As in the earlier Joint Stock plays there is a movement away from constraint towards the freeing of possi-bilities. This time it happens very early in the action and without previous preparation. Frequently, Churchill presents time as an elastic process which can be shaped and altered. Briefly in *Light Shining*, and more fully in *Cloud Nine* and *Fen*, she examines the power of the present moment within which all past and future moments potentially exist.

Theatre is an ideal forum within which to explore the role that time plays in our lives because, within the actual and defined time-span of the performance, it can create many and varied timescales. Through its focus of energy in the present moment, theatre can seemingly halt the one-directional for-ward movement of time and reveal its amorphous quality. In *Light Shining* the Ranters celebrate the energizing fluidity of the present moment; *Cloud Nine* explores a new fluidity of gender and status, and the interrelationship of past and present;

61

and *Fen*, the flux of varied levels of time and of consciousness. In *A Mouthful of Birds* the dancing, elusive figure of Dionysos begins and ends the action. Like the play, theatre is itself a stepping aside from reality. Dionysos, the androgynous, many-natured god epitomizes the fluid, transformative energy that is theatre. The undefended day is an exploration both of the characters' capacity for Dionysiac ecstasy and transformation, and of the related power of theatre.

3

The Radio Plays

Caryl Churchill's first work to receive professional performance was a group of radio plays, broadcast by the B.B.C. Third Programme between 1962 and 1973. An earlier play, *You've No Need to be Frightened*, was given a student production in 1961. Almost all of these plays deal, in one way or other, with the perturbing nature of change. The characters are frequently remote from the outside world, enclosed within static environments, which protect them from hostile external forces.

Radio is an excellent medium for expressing a sense of isolation. The action takes place within the mind of the listener, who is frequently alone, cut off from other people. In *You've No Need to be Frightened* the separateness of the individual listener has direct relevance to the play's subject matter. John, an elderly man, and his unnamed wife view the entities which make up their world from different and irreconcilable angles of perception. The woman sees only the familiar and comforting domestic objects which surround her, whereas his gaze is fixed on the snowy summit of a nearby mountain which seems to touch the stars. At the beginning of the play the woman is alone in the house. It is night-time, and she strains to make out the shape of her husband in the dark garden. She calls his name, but receives no reply. When John speaks, it is to a companion, a young guest who remains silent throughout the play. As John talks, he builds up a picture of his wife, so that the listener mentally joins the silent guest and sees the light in the window of the house, and the 'dark shape with a pale face looking out'. The woman is doing the washing up, as she does every night, and the husband describes her fingers, which 'will be all crinkly in the water'. To begin with the woman is distant and featureless, but this precise physical detail brings her into close-up.

Though this is a play for voices, it seems right to discuss it in visual terms. The two characters embody different ways of seeing, both of tangible realities and of what is important. He longs to leave behind everything that is known and certain, and to climb the mountain. He would go up above the treeline, and look down and see the tree-tops: 'all green and cold, like music it'd be to go up there.' Still he would continue climbing, towards the snow and the stars at the summit, and then perhaps, instead of returning, he would go on, down the far side of the mountain. The woman also sees the world in distinct colours, but, in contrast to the whiteness of snow and the green of the trees, she talks of the blackness and creamy brown of coffee in blue cups and the yellow of the kitchen curtains, the gaiety and warmth of which mingle with the morning sun. The man's gaze is fixed always on the distance and on things he has never seen; the woman's on the near-at-hand and the joy of ordinary domestic things. She bakes bread from locally milled flour and tends her chickens and goats. She sees that the stars and the mountain are beautiful, but has no wish to visit them. Even if her husband climbs to the summit, she tells their guest, he won't reach the stars. The 'mountains aren't all that high'.

Both husband and wife complain of their inability to make contact with each other. Each shuts out the other by the exclusiveness of their concerns. As John and his silent fellow witness watch the wife at the beginning of the play, he describes her actions as she slowly washes a large blue bowl 'round and round . . . in the dirty water with such love in her fingers'. Then she wipes it slowly and carefully. 'You can't reach her when she's doing that, she holds that bowl like a child.' He wishes that she was not so interested in domestic things, and the wife in her turn feels unable to 'get at' her husband when he is concentrating on the mountain and the stars. Each of them, however, recalls a past moment when they felt themselves to be included by the other. The man remembers his wife when she was young and beautiful. She would sit sewing in the lamplight, and he would feel unable to touch her.

But then she'd look up and smile and it was all right, like it was me in that material and everything when she loved it.

64

The wife tells the visitor that in a recent storm she was woken up by thunder and lightning and saw 'the room all lit up like the end of the world'. In her fear she reached out to her husband and he comforted her. 'You've no need to be frightened with me beside you', he said, and she fell securely asleep again.

These moments of contact are not enough in themselves to effect a change in the characters' situation. The catalyst which enables them to progress from their state of stasis is a small boy from a nearby village who comes to ask their help for his sick father. John and his wife both want to be the one to go, but in the end it is John who sets off, wearing his thick coat although winter has not yet begun. The wife tells the guest that he needn't stay until her husband returns. So long as John believes that she is not alone, he will not worry about her, and will feel free, after he has helped the sick man, to continue on up the mountain, and perhaps he will not return.

Throughout the play each of the two characters tries in turn to bring the visitor round to his or her way of viewing things. As the play progresses, the listener becomes one with the silent guest, seeing the world of the play first from one angle of perception, and then from the other. The result is evocative and at times very beautiful, but the play's structure does not lend itself easily to the expression of change. Despite John's departure and his wife's new-found ability to let him go, the still, elegiac quality continues through to the end of the play.

The Ants (broadcast in 1962) was Caryl Churchill's first play to be performed professionally. She originally intended it as a television play, but her agent, Margaret Ramsay, realized how ideally suited it was to radio. There are two central characters, the Grandfather and a little boy called Tim. Tim and his mother are staying with the Grandfather at his house by the sea, and the action takes place on the verandah of the house, overlooking the beach. Like the setting for *You've No Need to be Frightened*, this is an isolated place, and the rest of the world seems very far away. 'Nothing happens', says the Grandfather.

> The days drop into the sea out there . . . plop, plop, as the sun drops into the horizon.

In the distance, however, there is violence both personal and international. Though Tim does not know this, his parents are in the process of getting a divorce. He watches them as they walk on the beach and struggles to understand what they are saying, but they are too far away. Throughout the play he tries to make sense of a situation which he finds bewildering and potentially threatening. Much further away, so far in fact that Tim can scarcely comprehend it, a terrible war is being fought. Their side has just dropped a huge bomb and killed ten thousand of the enemy, but the event is unreal, difficult to take in. It has no effect on the concerns of Tim's parents, and his grandfather reads the news from the paper, where it is simply one sensational headline among many.

> Ten thousand dead. Well. Typist to wed Maharajah. President's dog has puppies. Backs are in fashion. Duke jumps in fountain. My Desire at 100–1. Nothing in the paper.

The Ants is a near perfect radio play, but it is easy to see why its author should have originally conceived it as a television piece. Even more strongly than *You've No Need to be Frightened* it lends itself to discussion in terms of close-ups and long distance shots. The central unifying image is that of the ants, and, with a small child's sense of detail for things that are near-at-hand, Tim presents them to the listener at the beginning in magnified form. He talks to them individually as they scurry to and fro, identifying them by what they are carrying and by their sizes, and focusing on his special favourite whom he has named Bill.

The little boy gives the ants individual characteristics, but the Grandfather compares human beings to identical ants, rushing greedily and pointlessly here and there. He reads from the newspaper about the bomb which has been dropped and asks Tim how many ants there are on the verandah. Ten thousand perhaps? If one looks at people from the top of a high building, they are simply little moving dots, just like ants. From an aeroplane even the dots vanish: there are only 'funny little toy towns, coloured targets'. Once the people have become invisible, it is quite easy to drop bombs on the unreal little toy-world.

66

The very vastness of the number of the dead helps to render them invisible. The newspaper headlines depersonalize the horror of the bombings: 'Ten thousand dead . . . Nothing in the paper.'

Now that the Grandfather is an old man and no longer the centre of anyone's world, he often finds it difficult to care very much about other people. When he was younger, he left Tim's grandmother. It's best not to love people, he tells the child, then you don't run the risk of betraying them. 'Desertion', he explains, 'is when you stop loving people and see them from miles above, when you lose them and see just a lot of black ants.' As the play progresses the ants come to represent the victims both of war and desertion, seen from far away as though through the wrong end of a telescope, and also all that Tim cannot understand and is threatened by. Though he is too young to take in very much of what he is told about the war and believes that it must be right to kill as many of the enemy as possible, the far off violence becomes confused with his friends the ants.

At the beginning Tim differentiates between the ants through variations in their sizes: 'You're little, you're little, you're middle, you're big', and this gives him a sense of security with regard to them. His parents by contrast perturb and disorientate him. They appear and disappear, sometimes with alarming rapidity, and seem at times to diminish and increase in size like Looking-Glass characters. Tim watches their tiny, distant figures as they walk on the beach and tries vainly to make out what they are saying to each other. Then they disappear behind some sand-dunes only to reappear suddenly to the child, and his excited description, as they approach closer and closer to the house, creates the illusion for the listener that they are growing in size.

Now I can't see them, they've come on to the road. They're nearly here, they're just coming along the road . . . They're at the gate, they're coming up the steps from the road. Here they are now, here they are!

As Tim becomes more disturbed and unhappy about the relationship between his parents, the friendly ants also become

67

alarming. At one point, he encourages the ants to crawl on his hand. At first there are only a few of them, and one is his friend Bill, so everything is all right. As he watches the ants, Tim tries to make sense of what his grandfather has told him about human beings deserting one another. 'Didn't you like Granny any more?' he asks. 'Daddy doesn't like us . . . He doesn't live with us.' The Grandfather asks Tim which of his parents he would prefer to live with, and at the same moment the little boy becomes conscious of the fact that there are dozens of ants swarming over his arms. They are menacing and uncontrollable like the strange new situation between the parents, and he screams and tries desperately to brush them off.

Near the end of the play, the now hugely threatening figures of the parents take over the action, quarrelling fiercely about custody in front of the child. When his mother begins to cry, Tim begs her not to and sobs: 'I hate you! Ant! Ant! Ant!' The parents go out, and the Grandfather also leaves temporarily, to try to find something with which to distract the boy. He tells Tim to count the time which elapses between the flashes from the lighthouse while he waits. Left alone, Tim struggles desperately to control his panic and grief.

> You ant you. Live by myself. I'll fly in a plane. There it is. One, two, three. You go away. Four five. One, two. I'll fly away in a plane. Don't cry, I hate you. One two three four five.

The Grandfather returns, pours petrol on to the ants, and prepares to set light to them. At the beginning of the play Tim reacts with distress when his mother suggests getting rid of the ants in this way. At the end he watches his grandfather place a piece of string in the petrol. Then the two of them crouch down, to watch from a distance as the string burns 'all the way down to the enemy'. The petrol bursts into flames, and Tim 'shrieks with laughter.'

The scarcely changing setting, the focus on the two central characters, the resonance of the central image, and the moving simplicity of dialogue and action make *The Ants* ideally suited to the demands of radio. The empty landscape translates into a tabula rasa of the mind, upon which key figures and events can be placed. The mind's eye is the ideal magnifying and reducing lens, capable of viewing characters and actions in close-up or long distance. Most of the time the little boy is at the centre of the picture, but at times the anguished squabbling of the parents blots out everything else. The suffering of the child and his parents remain separate, as does that of the victims of the distant, never-explained war. In the remote world of the Grandfather's house, where nothing ever happens and 'The days drop into the sea', personal pain and grief are all-absorbing, the tribulations of others difficult to comprehend.

In the final moments of the play, however, some connection is made between isolated experiences of suffering. The ending is complex and resonant. Despite the fact that Tim learns to destroy what he fears and to distance himself from painful emotions, the burning of the ants, representatives of the victims of war and abandonment, brings far off suffering closer to the self-enclosed world of the Grandfather's house.

In two of the radio plays broadcast in 1971 (*Abortive* on 4 February and *Not . . . not . . . not . . . not . . . not enough oxygen* on 31 March) the characters again attempt to shut themselves off from external circumstances which they find threatening. The action of *Abortive* takes place in the bedroom, and briefly the garden, of Colin's and Roz's suburban home. The play begins with the sound of wind in the trees. It is a hot, stormy night, a little before dawn, and the intermittent sounds of wind and rain form an integral part of the sound-texture of the play. The listener is frequently conscious of the restlessly tossing trees outside the house, and the rain, when it comes, offers a promise of relief to the characters as well as to the parched ground. The play's title refers to its subject matter in a metaphorical as well as a literal sense. The two characters discuss Roz's recent abortion, but their actions and inconclusive conversation are also abortive in a variety of ways.

The disturbed weather echoes the inner state of the characters and the relationship between them. The sound of wind in the trees is followed by silence, and then a 'whimpery' protesting moan from Roz. Colin wants to make love, but she is unable to respond and this leads them to talk about the circumstances and implications of the abortion. As though they are unable to resist the temptation of scratching a scarcely-healed wound, they go over and over the same related points, and the dark, stormy pre-dawn time seems to stretch endlessly as if morning light will never come. The father of the aborted child was not Colin, but Billy, a man from a less privileged background whom they briefly befriended. The sexual contact between Billy and Roz began as rape, but ended differently, and, as husband and wife probe their responses to Billy and the abortion, they reveal the jagged gulf between them.

Billy never speaks. He is created through Roz's and Colin's memories of him. They repeat the contradictory stories he told them about his background and, as a result, one version of him is superimposed upon, and cancels out, another. One past event stands out for Colin.

An English scene so remarkable for its pale green that it seemed even at the time like a memory or indeed a photograph.

The incident he remembers was a picnic, one hot day in April. They had hired a rowing boat, and Billy was standing on the bank and hesitating to get in the boat because he had never been on the water before. Colin's little daughter, aged three, put out her hand to Billy and told him not to be afraid. He remembers that Billy's anxiety and the child's attempt at re-assurance brought him close to tears, but Roz comments that Billy must have been lying because he told her 'he'd worked his passage to South America.'

It is Roz's and Colin's reminiscences of their subsequent treatment of Billy which bring him most fully to life. They describe the way in which they invited him into their home, but then became unhappy with the arrangement and told him to leave. Billy continued to haunt the area, hanging around the station car park and pleading with Colin to be received back into their favour. Roz used to look out of the window and see him sleeping in a nearby field. One night he telephoned over and over again, 'Crying and saying he was going to kill himself'. They were obliged, Roz recalls, to take the 'phone off the hook, but then he rang the door bell and they foolishly let him in. He was drunk, or drugged, and he kept repeating that he loved them. Finally, Colin pulled him by his feet, 'on his stomach clutching at everything he passed', down the stairs, out of the front door, and 'with a horrible bump' down the steps, and along the drive 'clutching furrows in the gravel'.

Roz expresses no pity for Billy. She remembers kicking him off when he tried to grab hold of her ankles as Colin dragged him past. Her one concern was to get him out of the house without waking the children. Prior to this nocturnal visit, he had taken to coming into the garden. This didn't frighten her, she explains, but it did make her angry, because it meant that she couldn't walk freely under her own trees, and because Billy justified his intrusion through his love for them.

Billy is a potent force within the play, but he remains deliberately shadowy and indistinct. He is the unwanted intruder who has to be expelled at all costs. Roz and Colin have thrown him out of the house, but they are haunted by their memories of him, as they are by thoughts of Roz's abortion. At the end of the play Roz links Billy with the aborted foetus.

> I sometimes think . . . one of my children was so small, only an inch or so, so stupid, a mental age of eight weeks from conception, what sort of a mind is that? Even less of a person than Billy.

The perturbing memories, the sound of wind and rain, Roz's fits of weeping, sometimes abruptly cut short, sometimes helplessly protracted, the unsuccessful attempts at communication, all together give form to a raw and desperate grief at the violent termination of possibilities which had been created. Billy is like the never-to-be-born child, indistinct and difficult to understand, but also threatening and totally demanding. Like their relationship with Billy, Roz's and Colin's attempts to make contact are abortive. They are unable to make love, and their endless retracing of events drives them further apart. Only at one point do they really come together. Roz leaves the conversation, and goes out into the wind and rain of the garden. Colin follows her and there is a brief moment of tenderness and closeness. They return to the bedroom, and it is then Roz who wants to make love, and Colin who feels sad and unable to. 'I might as well have had the baby', says Roz. 'You see, you do want it,' Colin accuses, and she agrees: 'I do miss something', and begins to weep.

When dawn finally comes, neither of them has slept. The darkness and wind and rain have been superseded by sunlight. A hot summer's day is beginning, but it brings no real relief from the anguish of the night. The characters return from the garden, and their subsequent failure to make love are followed by three lengthy speeches, the first from Roz as she remembers the disorientating, yet on the whole pleasant, sensation of the injection prior to the abortion. By the end of the speech the wind and rain have stopped, and in the silence Colin describes the incident with Billy and the boat. During the subsequent pause the dawn chorus begins and this continues while Roz relives their forcible eviction of Billy from the house. The turmoil and pain do not end with the night, but continue on into the new day. They settle down to try to get some rest, but, even in the sunshine, Roz is afraid to go to sleep. Just as she is drifting off, she has a feeling, 'like in a nightmare, but with no content'. She is afraid 'something's about to happen'. Nothing is resolved.

Though the menace never takes clear form, it is always present. The eight week old creature that might have been a child, the relationship with Billy, the sad bickering, the unful-filled attempts to make love: everything is unsatisfactory, and uncompleted. Time progresses from night to morning and, though the memories criss-cross, moving chronologically back-wards and forwards, they provide an ever deepening insight into past events. The action therefore reaches a conclusion for the listener, a distillation of all the play's interconnected ideas. For the characters however there is no release. The anxiety is only temporarily suspended. Fears and guilts await the return of night and of sleep.

Roz's fear on the brink of sleep recalls John's wife in *You've No Need to be Frightened*, but this time there is no element of reassurance. She talks also in her final speech of a dream in which she was killed by an explosion. She seemed to be falling very slowly and 'Everything was unsteady and far away'. It is as though the distant war in *The Ants* has come nearer, invading dreams. In the next play to be broadcast on radio the characters are besieged in one small room by the violence which is now clearly evident all around them.

The time in *Not . . . not . . . not . . . not . . . not enough oxygen* is the end of the twentieth century; the place, Mick's room in the Londons. Outside, there is stench, haze and smoke from pollution and burning tower blocks. Groups of people whom Mick terms fanatics set fire to the buildings and to themselves, in protest at wars, famine and injustice. The parks that used to exist in London are now mostly mud, plants are rare, and what grass still exists is surrounded by high fences. Birds have disappeared from the city. An ecological disaster has overtaken the entire planet. Everywhere resources are scarce, and it is necessary to procure a licence before having a child. Some parts of the world have become epidemic areas.

Mick's room in a tower block is cramped, but it provides him with some measure of security. There are shops and other facilities in the building, so it is rarely necessary to go out. Movement in the streets is difficult and dangerous. Cars are not allowed into the Londons without a permit, and buses move very slowly because of traffic jams and poor visibility. It is unwise to walk because of the possibility of meeting fanatics. The water supply in the room is inadequate, and it is difficult to breathe because of the lack of oxygen. Vivian, Mick's young mistress, speaks in desperate gasps, and from time to time sprays oxygen round the room to provide them with some measure of relief. She and Mick pass the time by doing puzzles and watching television. Occasionally they go up to the roof and walk about, but even there the air is hazy and unhealthy.

At the beginning of the play Mick is waiting for the arrival of his son, Claude, a famous TV personality whom he has not seen for five years. He is excited at the prospect of meeting his son again, and hopes that Claude will give him enough money to enable him to fulfil his dream and escape to a cottage in the park. While they wait, Vivian looks out of the window, hoping to catch a glimpse of Claude through the murk, and sees to her amazement a small brown bird, which Mick identifies from her description as a sparrow. The incident leads him to remember the large number of birds there used to be in the city, not only pigeons, but blackbirds, starlings, bluetits. He saw them with

73

his 'own eyes wild in the gardens of the Londons long ago'. The bird seems a good omen, a sign of possible freedom.

As in *The Ants* and *Abortive*, the characters try to prevent external pain, uncertainty and violence from infiltrating their enclosed world. From the window Mick and Vivian can see the Londons burning and collapsing around them. The television news invades their hermetically sealed box, providing an insistent reminder of more distant horrors. The TV has also been Mick's only contact over the last few years with his son. Sometimes the need to touch Claude has been so great, that Mick would kneel down and kiss his face on the screen.

Unlike Billy in *Abortive*, Claude is not a threatening intruder, but a longed for presence, a figure from the outside world who will enter the suffocating room and offer them help and comfort. When he finally arrives, however, Mick and Vivian learn that he has given away all his money, and plans to join the fanatics and kill himself. Vivian is concerned that he has come to murder them, but, after the first sense of shock, her main response is one of relief. She has always known that the nightmare external events would eventually penetrate into the room, and that some day:

> fanatic – fanatic would come and kill – always saying millions dying – hunger – dying – war – hunger – war every day so we kill – die – kill too and shock – shock – shock into stopping –

She has constantly tried to switch off the television news, so that she didn't have to know what was going on, but now she is glad that she can't do this anymore, and that the waiting is over.

Claude, the welcomed figure from the outside world, brings external suffering and violence into the room, but, in the event, he offers no threat to Vivian or his father. His anger and horror at a lunatic, uncaring world are turned upon himself. Through Claude's conversation with Mick, the listener learns about other members of their family. The wife of Mick's elder son, Alexander, had an unlicensed child, but the parents later killed it out of a sense of guilt. They were sentenced to five years' imprisonment for evading abortion, but this was suspended as the child was dead. They are now working as doctors in an epidemic area. Mick's wife left the Londons some time ago to roam about the countryside and live as best she could. She never learned to ignore the terrible images on the news and was eventually unable to shut herself off from the outside world any longer. Mick recalls that the news was always bad, even in the sixties, seventies and eighties. One had to be able to watch pictures of starving children and still eat one's dinner. It was the only way to survive.

Not . . . enough oxygen is a deeply disturbing parable of our time. The ecological destruction, the famine and wars, the determination to isolate oneself from horror and pain – all these are characteristics of our present-day world. Despite the bleakness of the vision, the play does contain hopeful elements. Vivian comes to some sort of recognition of the claims of other people's pain, and, though she fails to escape from the airless room, there is also the unheard, but powerfully suggested character of the wife. In *You've No Need to be Frightened* it is the husband who sets off for the mountain. Here it is the woman who has left, not for a distant and possibly unattainable goal, but as an expression of revulsion with an uncaring society. Claude's actions are a further form of protest. Destruction is much closer in *Not . . . enough oxygen*, but there are also stirrings of movement out of the sealed box.

In *Not . . . enough oxygen* there are few ways out because the surrounding devastation is so complete. It is possible to emerge from one's refuge, and to embrace danger or death, but not to change the situation. An earlier radio piece, *Identical Twins*, is a play for two voices. Clive and Teddy hate, and long to be free of, each other. They frequently speak simultaneously, and this, plus the similarity of their thoughts, creates the sense of a single, but dissociated consciousness. In the B.B.C. production both characters were played by the same actor. At the beginning of the play the twins have not met for ten years, and in the meantime they have tried to forge distinct identities. Teddy lives in London, where he derives his income from letting property. Clive owns a farm in the country. Their domestic situations, however, duplicate one another. Both are married with two children, both have mistresses.

Linked ideas of ownership, guilt and a determination to

escape from a restrictive situation run through the play. Clive has been finding it difficult for some time to watch any kind of suffering. He still sends the bullocks off to market, but, if he finds a fly on its back, he leaves it 'buzzing and turning' because he can't bear to tread on it. He recalls a horrifying incident when he ran over a dog. The body was under the car, but the head was still visible, and making dreadful noises because of the pain. He couldn't bring himself to put it out of its misery, and had to plead with his wife to do it instead. In a speech reminiscent of one of Cobbe's in *Light Shining in Buckinghamshire* Teddy describes how he once gave all his money to an old, half-blind matchseller. In the taxi afterwards he had no money to pay for his fare, and he thrust his watch at the driver and said, 'Bless you, my man. My wife is dead', in order to account for his behaviour by seeming 'mad or distracted with grief'.

Despite any sympathy and guilt they might feel at the sight of suffering, Clive and Teddy are determined not to let this stand in the way of whatever they want to achieve. Teddy's mistress Dawn is also his tenant, and he alternately toys with the idea of evicting her along with her husband and children, or allowing her to stay and enticing her husband on to a balcony which is unsafe. When Clive's wife makes the latest in a series of suicide attempts, Clive allows her to die, so that he can live with his mistress. Eventually, Clive is unable to cope any longer with the guilt of what he has done, and he takes an overdose of sleeping pills. Teddy does nothing to prevent his death, and inherits both the farm and Clive's mistress. He realizes, however, that he, in his turn, will probably commit suicide.

Just before Clive's death, the twins jointly remember a time when they were very small, and they looked into their mother's triple mirror. The two of them speak together, but Clive's voice is merely a whisper.

If we stood very close we could almost shut it round us. There were hundreds of reflections, all the same. (Clive's voice gets fainter.) Then I was terrified to move.

These are Clive's last words. Initially it seems that his death might allow Teddy to break free of the prison of reflected self-images, but it is clear by the end of the play that Teddy's subsequent actions are likely to be identical to Clive's.

The simultaneous speeches, the identical nature of the twins and the repetition of similar events create a kind of hall of mirrors from which the characters are unable to escape. Each of them is determined to be free, regardless of the cost, but their struggles only serve to imprison them further. In two late radio plays, *Schreber's Nervous Illness* and *Henry's Past*, the central characters find new ways of relating to experience, and, particularly in the latter play, a resulting freedom from restriction.

Schreber's Nervous Illness (1972) is adapted from the memoirs of Daniel Schreber. In 1893, at a relatively young age for such a high office, Schreber was appointed President of the Court of Appeal at Dresden. The strain of having to preside over judges who were considerably older than himself, and who understood court procedure better, made him unable to sleep, and caused an aggravated return of earlier symptoms of mental ill-health. He was admitted to the clinic of Professor Flechsig, and later transferred to the asylum at Sonnenstein. There, he would sit for long stretches of time completely immobile. He found it difficult to breathe, and was frequently unable to eat or defecate. He heard voices and suffered from hallucinations. Eventually, he recovered sufficiently to hold a coherent conversation and to play chess and the piano, although he was also subject to fits of bellowing. The original order of placement in the asylum had been only temporary, and he began to work for his discharge. His early attempts were unsuccessful, and in 1902 the order was made permanent. As a last resort he approached the Court of Appeal at Dresden of which he had formerly been president. The result was that he was found insane but capable of managing his affairs, and the committal order was revoked.

The play takes the form of a monologue, intercut with factual statements and the messages of the 'rays'. Schreber, previously an unbeliever, becomes convinced that God exists in the form of divine nerve rays which are constantly streaming into his body against their will. As God is used to dealing only with corpses, whose nerves he draws 'up to himself', Schreber remains motionless for hours on end. In this way he believes he is able to 'attract . . . impure souls . . . and by destroying them

. . . give God more power in the sky.' He is certain that he is the last person left alive and that the doctors and patients are 'fleeting-improvised-men' who are created miraculously and dissolve when they leave his presence. He is constantly assailed by the voices of the rays, who prevent him from getting any rest. These are divine nerve rays that have been misappropriated by Flechsig, who is also plotting against him in other ways. Schreber becomes convinced that he is changing into a woman, and decides that it is God's purpose, when he is unmanned, to use him 'to repopulate the world'. Flechsig intends to prevent this and to hand Schreber's 'female body . . . over to someone for sexual misuse'.

At first Schreber resists the physical changes that he sees happening to him, but he eventually gives in and surrenders himself to what he terms 'female voluptuousness'. Gradually he comes to accept that other human beings exist. The rays continue their incessant talk, but what they say is now nonsensical and less threatening. He is allowed to leave the asylum for short periods unaccompanied, and buys ribbons and cheap necklaces to adorn his body and 'to create a certain impression on God'. By the time of his discharge he has come to realize that 'despite strong indications of femaleness', he will probably 'die a man'. He alternates between a state of voluptuousness and sharp attacks of physical pain. He can usually prevent himself from bellowing by counting or engaging in some other occupation. When he is walking alone in the countryside, he makes things easy for himself and 'simply let[s] the bellowing happen'. By the end of the play Schreber has been through a process which is at least partially healing. His acquiescence in the changes that he imagines his body to be undergoing helps him to gain his freedom from the asylum, and gives him some sense of ease with his newly discovered self.

In *Henry's Past* the problems and possibilities of change are linked to the nature of time. Henry constantly re-examines a crucial moment from the past. Thirteen years previously he came to the conclusion, which may or may not have been justified, that his friend Geoffrey was also his wife's lover. He attacked Geoffrey and pursued him on to a fire escape where he hit him with a hammer. Geoffrey fell and broke his back and

Henry spent three years in prison. While he was inside, his wife, Alice, left him, taking with her their small daughter, and married Geoffrey. After his release, Henry began a relationship with Paulina, an old friend of his and Alice's. Henry lives constantly either in the past or the future, and this has become a way of obliterating the present moment. He mulls over events in his past life as though this persistent reappraisal might provide him with the key to understanding what really happened and why. Memories, though vivid and painful, are not always reliable and he is at times uncertain of the exact sequence of events. Motivation is particularly difficult to pin down. When his mind is not occupied with the past it is taken up with anticipation of the occasional visits, from their new home in Canada, of his daughter, and Alice and Geoffrey. When they arrive, however, the present moment still eludes him. It lacks the vibrancy and reality of the past.

> I watch them talk, sit, stand. I see their ears, fingers, wisps of hair. That is Alice. That is Geoffrey. That girl is my daughter. They pass, they pass.

In order to provide himself with a new audience on whom to try out his various versions of the past, he brings home a young unmarried mother named Silvy. She also has a past with which she is trying in a somewhat incoherent way to come to terms. Should she leave the baby with his foster parents, or bring him up herself? Henry offers to marry her if she reclaims the baby, but his interest never really engages with Silvy or her problems. She is a means of passing the time until the arrival of Alice, and a convenient excuse for the retelling of his story. As though he were showing her photographs in an album, he reanimates previous happenings: Alice cooking at the stove on the night that he first suspected her of infidelity, the heavy downpour which seemed to batter him from all directions as he came out of the prison gates, making him feel giddy and in danger of losing his balance.

Like Henry, Alice also retains vivid mental images of the past, but she is undisturbed by their randomness. She finds the past fascinating in a similar way to the 'fragments from

79

an archaeological site'. What survives and what does not is arbitrary. In her new life with Geoffrey she has become a well-known photographer, transfixing 'forever the fleeting moment'.

At the end of the play Henry moves tentatively towards a recognition of the validity of the present as the characters relive past incidents, unconnected with the traumatic events of thirteen years ago. Geoffrey remembers the joy of running as a child, and lying afterwards in a garden 'full of roses'. Alice recalls things that her lover has told her about his childhood, and Lydia talks of her sense of disbelief at seeing a view of the English countryside that looked just like a picture postcard. 'It hardly seem[ed] true.' This leads Paulina to describe 'standing on a ruined tower', in which county she can no longer recall, and watching swallows 'flashing past', dark against the pale sky. In turn, Silvy brings to mind swallows in the roof of her aunt's house in Devon. All the separate images are linked through a web of correspondences. Each overlaps the other, and the past, which was once the present, is recognized and valued. Henry's final words hesitantly affirm the connection between then and now, 'Do you know . . . just then . . . now . . . then . . . is the present moment.'

The radio plays are not to be viewed as simply a form of apprenticeship for the later stage plays. Each amply repays study in its own right, and some are amongst the most powerful and moving examples of Caryl Churchill's work. In the way in which they document both a desire for change and the obstacles which prevent it they do, however, represent a first step towards the later plays of transformation and awakened possibilities. The characters are imprisoned within their closed environments through fear of the outside world, an unwillingness to come face to face with the inequity and suffering which surround them, and a sense of powerlessness. The distant violence in *The Ants* becomes the formless but ever-present menace in *Abortive*. In *Not . . . enough oxygen* it has burrowed its way into the heart of the characters' sanctuary. Clive and Teddy in *Identical Twins* struggle unsuccessfully to fight their way out of the multiple reflections which imprison them, but in *Schreber's Nervous Illness*, Schreber's surrender to the forces

OWNERS: Royal Court Theatre Upstairs, London, 1972.

LIGHT SHINING IN BUCKINGHAMSHIRE:
Royal Court Theatre Upstairs, London, 1976.

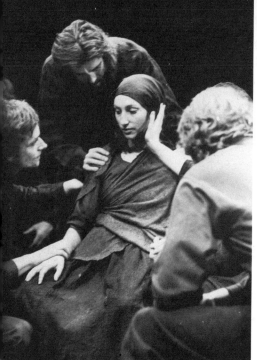

LIGHT SHINING IN
BUCKINGHAMSHIRE:
Royal Court Theatre Upstairs,
London, 1976.

CLOUD NINE:
Royal Court Theatre,
London, 1979,

CLOUD NINE: Royal Court Theatre, London, 1980.

CLOUD NINE: Royal Court Theatre, London, 1979.

TOP GIRLS: Royal Court Theatre, London, 1982.

TOP GIRLS: Royal Court Theatre, London, 1982.

FEN: Almeida Theatre, London, 1983.

SERIOUS MONEY: Royal Court Theatre, London, 1987.

within and around him gives him a measure of freedom and recovery. Henry in *Henry's Past* lacks the ability to live in the present. He is like a traveller in a time capsule which is stuck always in the past and the future, never the 'now'. Like the characters in their static enclosed worlds, he too is a prisoner. His release comes from his understanding of the relatedness of moments of intense feeling in the past to everything that is actual and potential within the present moment. The characters in the majority of the radio plays fear connectedness and struggle to prevent it. Henry's freedom, as so often in Churchill's stage plays, comes through a recognition of the unity of then and now, and of the beneficient forces which exist within the present moment.

4

Possibilities Realized and Denied

Churchill's preoccupation with the nature of time is particularly acute in two plays of the mid seventies: *Traps* and a science fiction play, *Moving Clocks Go Slow*.

The first scene of *Moving Clocks Go Slow* takes place on a scan station in space, the next four on planet earth, and the final one in a black hole. Earth has become the slum of the universe. All its resources have been used up, and little is left but crumbling buildings and mounds of rubbish. In the early days of space exploration, outward was a colony of earth, but, as the situation on their home planet worsened, the early explorers chose not to return. Now only specials, human beings with outstanding extra-sensory powers, are allowed to leave earth. outward is inhabited by specials, non-human life forms, and sophisticated robots known as Pals (psychokinetic android labourers). The continued existence of earth remains important to outward because, like death, it makes almost any condition of life seem bearable by comparison.

> Demotion to earth is a real fear. There are places so cold and bleak, you can't step out. But earth is still the bottom. Earthing is the end.

The representative of outward on earth is Agent Fox, a huge, cumbersome special, whose body consists almost entirely of transplants. Fox controls earth by 'balancing terror and gratitude'. He creates wars and famines, then outward rushes aid to the stricken areas. There are constant lotteries which affect almost every aspect of life, and which provide some sense of hope and excitement to relieve the bleakness of human existence.

In order to prevent its inhabitants from escaping, earth is ringed with scan stations, where applicants are monitored before being processed outward. Kay has worked on one of these stations for fifteen years but has aged only three years in the process. She was one of the last people to qualify for her post. She is not a special, and cannot journey outward, but she is grateful not to be on earth, and proud to 'Serve space'. In the first scene of the play Fox visits Kay's station to warn her that aliens are streaming through a black hole and infiltrating earth. He gives her permission to detonate the station if she has reason to suspect the presence of aliens, but explains that they are difficult to detect, as they are not composed of matter. In the event, a special and a Pal are killed, and then reanimated by aliens who have taken over their bodies. They leave for earth, taking Kay with them to prevent her from activating the alarm, and also as a guide to human behaviour.

The aliens are without form or senses, and need to inhabit human bodies in order to experience earth. The alien who takes over the body of a special called Apollo, at first finds the human structure and ways of responding to external stimuli difficult to adjust to. Skin encases him, 'little chinks of eyes and ears' let in only a fraction of 'the waves' he knows to be all around him. With practice, however, he comes to delight in the body's possibilities, its easy capacity for movement, and the way in which thoughts come out of the mouth as words.

On earth Kay meets up with her daughter Stella, who looks the same age as herself, and her mother Mrs. Provis, an elderly tramp who had the necessary gifts to be recognized as a special, but who chose to stay on earth. The play centres round the relationship between the three generations of women, and explores the fluid nature of time and the simultaneous existence of many kinds of possibilities. In the first scene of the second act the three women, together with Apollo and a friend of Kay's called Rocket, leave London, where they have been living, and walk along the remnants of an old road. Apollo talks about the distinctive quality of time in his universe: it 'isn't one thing after another . . . . It's all available at once', like the human concept of space. The road jolts Kay's and Mrs. Provis's memories of other times. Mrs. Provis remembers riding in a blue Ford Cortina car when she was a little girl, and Kay points out the relics of a railway line. 'There should be metal rails and a train.' The ruined buildings nearby should be houses with people in them. Later they sit by the roadside and relax, and Kay is visited by the sense that she is doing something that she has done before, 'the feeling of time having slipped'. They hear the distant sound of a car, which grows gradually louder, and they are alarmed and bewildered because there is no longer any metal with which to build cars, or petrol to fuel them. The others are unsure of what exactly they have heard and seen, but Mrs. Provis describes a blue Ford car, with a small girl in the back, waving, and she remembers a day in her childhood.

In the blue Ford. Kneeling on the back seat looking out of the window. Waving to some people by the road. And one of them was an old tramp. Me. That was me waving to me.

The little girl in the car comes from a time before Stella or Kay were born, and before the earth's resources were wantonly destroyed. Time takes on something of the complexity which Apollo described. Aliens are now streaming to earth thick and fast, and Apollo can hear that the air is full of many, varied sounds: 'Different kinds of rustle'. The present moment is charged with possibilities, which could be hostile or healing. Mrs. Provis draws their attention to the wonder of the sky above their heads, and, when Rocket replies with the conventional slogan, 'Look outward', Stella corrects him: 'No, sky for once.' Her words are followed by the voice of a railway announcer, an echo from the ruined station nearby, and the sound of a train which comes closer and then fades into the distance. Fragments of the past interweave with the present.

The following scene takes place in the same location. The sun is shining, but Kay sits very still because she is afraid that, if she moves, she 'might jog something'.

The air's full of change. One more thing could precipitate – what? The sky might craze like glass.

Time however continues to slip and slide. Characters repeat lines of dialogue without any indication that their words are not new. First Stella and then Kay, begin to speak like small children, as they relive past moments of betrayal by their respective mothers. When the present moment reassembles, they are able to talk openly to each other for the first time. Kay, the mother of Stella and the daughter of Mrs. Provis, quietly describes opportunities for loving which once existed, but which came to nothing. Until this point in the play she has been the most closed off of the three women. In her neat white capsule of a scan station she worked efficiently and obsessionally, entirely taken up with her wish to 'Serve space'. On earth she felt little sympathy or affection for her mother or her daughter. She spent her time in London hunting through the mounds of refuse, trying to find items of furniture with which to construct a home round herself as a protection from the outside world. Now, for the first time, Kay allows the present moment to expand or contract at will, and lets in memories of past failures and inadequacies. She recognizes that, though she likes her mother, it is too late now to learn to love her. She could once have loved baby Stella, but the opportunity was wasted. In a similar way the possibility of cultivating and caring for the earth has been thrown away. It could, says Stella:

> be thick with vegetables. There could be water that didn't taste of metal. It's just a little planet wasted.

The final moments of the play take place in darkness. Earth has been detonated by outward because it is saturated with aliens. The voices of Apollo, an alien who has taken over a Pal called Luna, and Kay are heard as they spin through a black hole which will take them through to another universe. Kay wants to return to earth, and the other two explain to her that the only possible way is by 'connecting with a different time'. In the dimension which they have now entered 'Space is one way'. Kay's voice ceases, and that of Apollo is heard describing her whereabouts to Luna. Kay has gone back in time, and returned to earth before it was blown up. Now she is 'On a rubbishy plain', surrounded by 'Old tin cans and weeds'. Luna asks what she is doing, and Apollo replies:

Up on her feet. Walking. Something – what? Losing her now.
She's crying.

'Happy or sad?' asks Luna, but there is no reply and her
question ends the play. Kay has returned to an earlier point in
her existence, and that of earth, but what she will make of this
remains uncertain.

In the opening moments of *Traps* a woman walks to and fro in
a cluttered, dimly lit room, with a baby on her shoulder, trying
to get it to sleep. A man sits in a chair with his eyes closed.
Downstairs, a dog barks, and the woman reacts anxiously in
case the sound wakes the child. A second man, his clothes wet
from the rain which is pouring down outside, comes noisily into
the room, and puts on the light. He realizes that the baby is
asleep and quietly turns the light off again. The woman puts the
baby into a carrycot and goes out with it. The man switches on
the light, takes off his wet things and begins to talk. The man in
the chair takes no notice.

The beginning of a play provides an audience with information which leads them, consciously or unconsciously, to set up
expectations as to what will happen next. In *Traps*, however,
this information is constantly reassessed and challenged. It is
itself a kind of trap, and the audience have to be constantly
alert, willing to go in whatever direction the action takes them.
In a brief foreword to the play, Churchill describes it as a kind of
'impossible object', in which the characters live simultaneously
a number of the possibilities that are open to them. The
constantly changing motives and relationships have validity
only on stage, in life they would be impossible. There is,
however:

> no flashback, no fantasy, everything that happens is as real and
> solid as everything else within the play.

The three characters who are present at the beginning, Syl,
the woman with the baby; Jack, the seated man and Albert, the
figure who comes into the room, are later joined by three
others. Reg, the first of them to enter, is Jack's brother-in-law,

though at this point he is a stranger to Syl and Albert. His wife, Christie, has left him, and he thinks that she may have come to stay with Jack. Later Christie arrives, brought, Jack claims, by the fact that he has willed her to come; but, before this, they are joined by Del, who used to be a member of the group, but who left in imperfectly explained, unhappy circumstances. The characters live out a variety of possibilities, and one set of motivations and relationships merges neatly and seamlessly into another, like the strip of paper which Del twists and joins to form a Mobius strip (a loop with only one surface). Syl, for example, is married, alternately to Albert and to Jack, or at some points in the action involved with them both. Sometimes she has a child, or is pregnant, sometimes not. The characters explore different permutations of sexual and emotional alliances, and whichever exists at the moment erases all previous and subsequent liaisons.

Of the three characters who enter later in the action, Christie, through her kinship with Jack, is the one who is most easily integrated into the group. Despite his earlier involvement with the other characters, Del, like Reg, is an outsider. Both men have a considerable capacity for violence and this is frequently linked in some way with Christie. Reg physically abuses Christie in a number of the possible relationships which potentially exist between them, and at the beginning of Act Two Del tells her about a rape and murder which he claims to have committed in the belief that she will understand his motivation. In the first act Del makes two entrances, and the second, which is a replica of the first, is played as if it is happening for the first time. Del is filled with anger because of the unfair way that he believes he has been treated in the past, but the reactions of the other characters are different each time, and this alters what follows. The fury of Del's first entrance is diffused through the affection that the others show him, but the second time he interrupts an acrimonious interchange which centres round Reg and Christie, and his violence is fuelled by the atmosphere in the room. There is a physical struggle, and the others tell him to leave.

The constant shifts in relationships take place within a setting which, with only marginal modifications, remains the same throughout the play's two acts. The clock tells the real time, and, in spare moments, the characters work on a jigsaw which is almost complete by the end of the play. In this way the audience's sense of time as a linear progression is stressed, but complicated and contradicted by the changing and irreconcilable patterns of allegiances and motivations. Many of the objects in the play are subject to transformation, depending on the existing set of circumstances. Albert exits with a pile of clothes which Syl has ironed. Later he enters with the same clothes, now creased and damp, and begins to iron them himself, despite the fact that he earlier claimed never to do any ironing. At the end of Act One Del breaks a bowl of peas, and partially destroys a plant, but at the beginning of Act Two the bowl is unbroken and the plant is as it was at the beginning of the play. In the first act Jack locks the door and pockets the key to prevent Reg from leaving. Shortly afterwards, Albert goes out, without first unlocking the door, but, when Reg tries it, the door is locked once again.

Despite the almost identical setting, the first act takes place in a city, and the second in the country. There are references in the first act to an earlier, happier time in the country, but the second act could not be a flashback. Characters who meet for the first time in Act One are living together as a group in Act Two. The bowl which Del breaks at the end of Act One is a teasing addition to the play's complexities, as it is already broken when the play begins, and then mended by Albert before Del's entrance. It is like the baby whose existence or non-existence is dependent on Syl's circumstances, or the door which can open for one character and remain locked for another. The play's events twist in and out like a Mobius strip, presenting one unbroken surface. A character exits and then re-enters, as if for the first time. Del cuts his finger while he is preparing vegetables, and the same thing happens to Jack. At the beginning of the play Syl lulls the baby to sleep in the 'Bluish gloom of early evening'. In the middle of Act Two the same lighting state recurs, but it is succeeded by the diffused glow from an oil lamp, in place of the electric light of Act One, and this affects the characters' mood and behaviour. The prevailing atmosphere and the attitude of the others alter a person's motivation and actions.

In the final section of the play, the relationships change gear more frequently and sharply. Loving, creative possibilities are contrasted with moments of unhappiness and rejection. Reg and Christie begin to 'kiss and caress' each other, but their interest cools and each blames the other for the lack of feeling between them. Reg tells Christie that the best plan would be for them to part, and, when she pleads with him to change his mind, he knocks her to the floor and kicks her, and then begins to cry. Earlier in the act the characters have discussed Albert's recent suicide, but he enters at this point, his hands dirty and his boots caked with mud from gardening, and asks quite normally if he has missed supper. Jack comes in with a large tin bath, which Del and Syl fill with hot water, and each of the characters undresses in turn and gets into the bath, while the others assist by providing additional hot water and dry towels, or washing someone's back for them. Throughout, Reg is embarrassed and ill at ease, watching Christie out of the corner of his eye and declining to get into the water himself. The others gather round to eat, but Jack refuses to give Reg any food until he has bathed. Slowly and self-consciously, Reg gets into the water. Then, as Jack washes his back, he gradually relaxes and, for the first time, finds words to express the distress he felt when Christie left him.

> When I drove up in the rain looking for Christie I could hardly see the road in front of me. What with crying and the windscreen wipers not working properly. So I could hardly say I knew that road.

Jack puts some food onto a plate, and Reg asks if he can have it in the bath where he is warm and comfortable. Del hands him the plate, and, as they all continue with their meal, each of them gradually starts to smile. In the final seconds of the play Reg also begins to smile, and then to laugh.

The ritual of cleansing and sharing which ends the play has, in one sense, no greater claim to importance than any of the preceding possibilities which are explored. Del may channel his energies into a realization of the utopian dreams which are his equivalent of Albert's more politically orientated hopes, or squander them in mindless acts of violence. At the beginning of Act Two, Christie shows Del her back which is covered with bruises from Reg's ill-treatment of her, but when she gets into the bath at the end of the play her skin is unblemished. Both these eventualities exist for her, just as Albert may live or die, and Reg find a sense of community and release, or vent his anger and frustration through a destructive relationship with his wife.

Inevitably, however, the audience must, as the onstage clock reminds them, experience the various possibilities not simultaneously, but in sequence. We live within a constantly changing set of variables, which we structure into past, present and future. Though it explores many co-existing possibilities of choice, *Traps* is carefully fashioned. It would be theoretically possible to begin an examination of the Mobius strip of relationships at any point, but it makes dramatic sense to start with the three centrally related characters, and to raise, and then confuse, expectations about the relationship which exists between them. The many changes of direction and mood lead rhythmically and satisfyingly to the communal meal and to the smiles which light up the characters' faces. Time is a dual process throughout the performance of the play. The clock marks the linear progression of events, but the constant throwing up of new circumstances and possibilities of action turns time forward and backwards on itself, so that the celebration of the present moment, and of the caring relationship between all the characters which it potentially contains, becomes capable of realization in the final moments of the play.

Its affirmation of creative possibilities links *Traps* with *Henry's Past* and *Light Shining in Buckinghamshire*. In *Light Shining*, which was written shortly before *Traps*, the climax of the play is the sacramental union of the Ranters, through the sharing of food and physical contact – a utopian vision in the midst of the stark realities of privation and lack of freedom which surround them. Reg's laughter as he sits eating food in the bath is reminiscent of Brotherton allowing herself to be touched in *Light Shining*. It is a kind of baptism into a world of new possibilities. The word utopia, as Del reminds the other characters, literally means 'nowhere'. *Traps* makes sense only in its own terms. The proliferation of possibilities which results in a communal sense of ease and happiness can exist in this form only within the world of the play.

The utopian possibilities which *Light Shining in Buckinghamshire* explores are forcibly terminated by the restoration of a hierarchical society and a legal system based primarily on the rights of property. Churchill's interest in time and the possibilities of change is enriched and highlighted by her focus, in a number of her plays, on external restrictions of freedom, and on an aggressive individualism which prevents constructive change and works against the good of society as a whole. The title of her first play to receive a professional stage production, *Owners* (Royal Court Theatre Upstairs, December 1972) reveals its central theme. Churchill's twin starting points for the eighteen short scenes, which shift abruptly in style between the naturalistic and the hilariously grotesque, were the relationship between landlord and tenant, and the contrast between an 'active, achieving' form of Christianity, and Eastern passivity, characterized by the words:

Onward Christian Soldiers,
Marching as to war.

Christian hymn

and

Sitting quietly, doing nothing.
Spring comes and the grass grows by itself.

Zen poem.

In order to avoid an oversimplified male/female distinction, the passive character is a man, and the central striving, achieving character is a woman. Marion is married to Clegg, owner of an unsuccessful butcher's shop. In the past she had a mental breakdown, and the hospital doctors tried to persuade her that sanity lay in being a conventional wife. Instead, she used a small inheritance, augmented by a loan from Clegg, to buy her first house. She has been speculating in property ever since. Alec, Marion's ex-lover, and his wife Lisa, along with their children and Alec's senile mother, are sitting tenants in Marion's latest purchase, and she sends an employee, Worsely, to bribe, or frighten them into leaving.

With the exception of Alec, all the characters, to one degree or another, see other people in terms of property. Clegg believes that husband and wife are 'one flesh', and that a husband should be the dominant partner in all aspects of marriage. He hates Marion's success, and her lack of subservience, and plots with Worsely bizarre ways of murdering her. Worsely makes constant, but unsuccessful offstage attempts to kill himself. With each successive, botched suicide attempt, he mutilates himself still further so that, by the end of the play, he is almost entirely encased in bandages. Worsely does genuinely try to end his life, it's just that circumstances are against him. He enlists the aid of the Samaritans, but, to his disgust, instead of helping, they try to prevent him from killing himself. 'Life is leasehold', one of them explains to him:

> It belongs to God the almighty landlord. You mustn't take your life because it's God's property not yours.

Alec and Marion represent the poles of passivity and acquisitiveness. Marion has struggled hard to reach her present level of success. Her favourite hymn when she was seven, was *Onward Christian Soldiers*, and she has learned from the Bible that human beings are the lords of creation.

> God gave him dominion over every beast of the field and fowl of the air. Gave the land to him and to his seed forever. Doesn't evolution say the same? Keep on, get better, be best. Onward. Fight.

There is a certain guilt attached to achieving and owning, but that is a spur to further success: 'what would happen to work without guilt?' Though her relationship with Alec ended some years earlier, she still wants him and believes that he belongs to her. She buys the house knowing that he lives in it, and as a way of getting at him.

Like Marion, Alec used to be interested in bettering himself and getting on in the world, but now he finds it difficult to want anything. He sits quietly: 'Doing nothing. The day goes by itself.' As he tells Marion, he is no longer even physically the person he was seven years earlier when they were having an affair. He has changed, 'Skin and all', in the intervening time.

His wife Lisa finds him incomprehensible. Her attitudes are a paler version of Marion's (Alec, the children, the household goods are all hers), but she is a more sympathetically presented character. Alec has given up his job, and she works for long hours in a hairdressing salon even though she is heavily pregnant. She is frightened by Worsely's threats regarding the house, and asks the advice of Marion, of whose ownership of the property she knows nothing. Her anger on discovering that Worsely is working for Marion is exacerbated when she walks in on Marion and Alec making love. She tells them that she has no intention of adding to her problems by looking after the baby. When it's born, Marion can take care of it, and see how well she manages to cope.

The baby has no existence for Marion in its own right. It is a piece of property with which to barter for the return of her old relationship with Alec. While Lisa is still weak from giving birth, Marion persuades her to sign over the guardianship of the baby, and is then deaf to all her pleas to return him. The child is her 'bit' of Alec, and no-one is going to take him from her. She buys Clegg a new butcher's shop. If Alec fails to see reason, they will keep the child, and one day their investment in it will mature. There will be a sign above the shop door, 'Clegg and Son', signifying a thriving business partnership.

The context in which the play's events occur, the use of terminology related to a butcher's shop and the ownership of property, and the juxtaposition of naturalistic and macabrely funny elements frequently throw a startling and unexpected light on conventional attitudes. The notion that a husband and wife are 'one flesh' takes on alarming connotations when the words are spoken by a butcher. Clegg sees both the women and the baby in terms of meat. Lisa is a 'Nice bit of rump. Marion's more like something for a stew. She's all gristle.' His adopted son is:

> . . . as nice a bit of little baby as you'll see. Turns the scales now at fifteen pounds, and I'm the one fattened him up . . .

The ramifications of ownership are extensive and complex. Most of the characters see love as essentially acquisitive, having and holding regardless of the wishes of the other. The idea that one human being can belong to another is most worrying in the context of the parent/child relationship. Near the end of the play, Worsely returns the baby to Lisa and Alec because that is where he 'belongs'. It is clearly the best solution. Marion does not love the baby, whereas his parents do. The word 'belong' has been subject to so much scrutiny by this point in the play, however, that, even in the context of restoring the child to the people who love him, it creates a certain sense of unease.

Owners does not suggest answers to the problems of emotional acquisitiveness, so much as bring into conjunction seemingly disparate elements in the hope that an audience will be amused and shocked into seeing accepted attitudes in a new light. Marion has no uncertainties about her actions. On her instructions, Worsely, at the end of the play, sets fire to the house while Alec and his family are in it. Worsely has just returned the baby, however, and it seems a waste to allow it to die, so he alerts them by shouting 'Fire'. They all get out safely, but then Alec remembers the presence of another baby, whom they had promised to look after for the new owners of the house, and he goes back into the building. Far from bringing Marion to her senses, Alec's death, and that of the second baby, make her realize what she might be capable of. She has referred to herself earlier as a man of destiny. At the end of the play she begins to discover just how ruthless and determined she can be. In the context of Churchill's recurring theme of the potential existence of new directions and possibilities, linked always to the circumstances of surrounding lives, Marion's moment of self-discovery is ironic. Her philosophy: 'Do what you want. Get what you can' negates the possibility of constructive change.

Like *Traps* and *Moving Clocks Go Slow*, *Top Girls* experiments with the idea of time. Like *Owners* it presents a central character who is determined to succeed, even if this means trampling on the needs of others. However, whereas the reversal of traditional roles in *Owners* is simply to liberate the qualities of passivity and aggression from gender-bound expectations, it is *essential* that Marlene, the main character in *Top Girls*, should be a woman.

The opening scene takes place in a restaurant, and the

mutability of time within the play is introduced through the fact that Marlene is celebrating her appointment as managing director of the Top Girls Employment Agency in the company of five famous women from the past. When the majority of her guests are assembled, Marlene toasts her own success, and theirs, with the words:

> . . . we've all come a long way. To our courage and the way we changed our lives and our extraordinary achievements.

As they eat and drink, the women ply each other with details of their astonishing lives. The stories overlap and interweave, so that one anecdote merges into, and enriches the pattern of the rest. Some of the experiences which they recall are horrific, and there are outbursts of anger at the restrictions and cruelties against which they had to struggle, but, overwhelmingly, the first scene is a celebration of achievement by women in the face of seemingly insurmountable odds. At the end of the scene, Isabella Bird, the nineteenth-century traveller, recalls the journey she made to North Africa when she was an old woman.

> So off I went to visit the Berber sheikhs in full blue trousers and great brass spurs. I was the only European woman ever to have seen the Emperor of Morocco. I was seventy years old. What lengths to go to for a last chance of joy.

The word 'joy' recurs in Churchill's work, linked with the realization of dormant possibilities. The opening scene places Marlene's success within a context of extraordinary achievements by women in the past, and raises expectations of a further celebration of the ways in which women have altered the course of their lives. Like her dinner guests, Marlene has shown great energy and resourcefulness. She may not have had to battle against odds as severe as theirs, but she has travelled a long way from her underprivileged origins. Instead of seeking out the opportunities for joy of which Isabella Bird speaks, however, she has concentrated her energies on climbing the capitalist ladder. There is a wider range of possibilities open to her than was available to these women from the past, but her horizons are narrower.

All except one of the central scenes take place in the employment agency, where Marlene and her colleagues interview candidates for top jobs. The exception is the last scene in Act One, which is set in the back yard of the house belonging to Marlene's sister, Joyce. Angie, Marlene's sixteen-year-old niece, and a younger friend called Kit are huddled together in a shelter they have built out of junk. The brief lines of dialogue revolve around Angie's sense of angry frustration and powerlessness. She bullies and taunts Kit, though she is clearly dependent on her affection, and refuses to obey her mother. Towards the end of the scene Joyce sends her into the house to tidy her bedroom, but, instead, Angie comes back out, wearing 'an old best dress', which is 'slightly small for her'. She has put it on, she tells Kit, in order to kill her mother.

The central scenes take place within a brief linear segment of time, which ends with Marlene's assessment of Angie's chances in a society of winners and losers. Angie has come up to London to visit Marlene, whom she suspects of being her real mother. She idolizes Marlene, and longs to be like her, but the hopelessness of these aspirations is made clear by Marlene's summing up: 'She's a bit thick. She's a bit funny . . . She's not going to make it.' Her words end the forward progression of time within the play, but they are followed by the long final scene, which predates the earlier ones by a year, and situates them within a wider and richer context.

In the last scene Marlene is visiting Joyce and Angie after a gap of six years, and she has brought with her a number of presents, including the dress that Angie wore at the end of Act One. Now, however, it is new, and the right size. Joyce and Marlene are never seen together until this final scene. Whereas Marlene has been determined to escape from the limitations of her background no matter what the cost, Joyce has remained in the place where she grew up, because she was both unable and unwilling to follow Marlene's example. The two women remain linked, however, by Angie, who is revealed in the course of an acrimonious discussion to be Marlene's daughter. Joyce, the elder sister, was married and childless when Marlene gave birth to Angie at the age of seventeen, and she offered to bring the baby up as her own child.

The passionate and angry debate between the sisters in the final scene widens outwards from a bitter exchange of recriminations regarding Angie, and recollections of the privations of their parents' lives to a statement of diametrically opposed views on Britain in the nineteen eighties. Marlene's go-getting, success-orientated philosophy is endorsed by Thatcherite economics. The eighties, she believes, are going to be a time of golden opportunity, when 'Anyone can do anything if they've got what it takes.' 'And if they haven't?' asks Joyce. If, like Angie, they lack the necessary intelligence, or energy, or resourcefulness, what then? A society which pays its top people handsome rewards cares little about the losers. Most lives are still wasted: 'nothing's changed for most people'.

In a more complex way than the first scene, the last one brings the present into connection with the past. *Top Girls* begins with a celebration of achievement by women and then contrasts Marlene's success story with the stories of other lives, particularly those of the two women to whom she is most intimately related. Marlene's values are the prevailing ones of her society, which constructs a hierarchy culminating in the top people. The only change from the past is that a small number of women can now scramble to the top of the ladder, alongside, and sometimes ahead of, men. Meanwhile, opportunities and lives are wasted as the earth and possibilities of love and affection were wasted in *Moving Clocks Go Slow*.

In the final moments of the play Angie comes downstairs to look for her mother, and finds Marlene who is settling down for the night. She is frightened, and Marlene asks if she has had a bad dream and tries unsuccessfully to reassure her. Angie's repetition of the word 'Frightening', which ends the play, is the summation of everything that Marlene has chosen to ignore in order to succeed. Angie's bewilderment and fear are seen to inform all the earlier events, and Marlene's assessment of her chances of success in life to have been made in the light of this encounter. By implication, Marlene stands for all top people, integrally connected, whether they accept the fact or not, with the have-nots of society, and Angie, the unacknowledged daughter, for the many unfulfilled lives which in Churchill's terms are of value, even if they seemingly achieve nothing.

Caryl Churchill followed *Top Girls* with two plays for the Joint Stock Theatre Group, *Fen* and *A Mouthful of Birds*. *Serious Money*, which opened at the Royal Court Theatre in March 1987, resembled the Joint Stock plays in having an initial workshop period. Thematically however, in its criticism of the selfish acquisitiveness of contemporary British society, it is more closely akin to *Owners* and *Top Girls*. Churchill returns frequently in her work to the uncaring nature of capitalism, but these three plays with their central focus on the owners, the top people, together constitute her most powerful indictment of the way in which capitalism operates in the nineteen seventies and eighties. Where *Owners* focuses on speculation in property and human lives, and *Top Girls* on the appropriation by women of traditional male attitudes and avenues to success, *Serious Money* revolves round financial dealings in the City, immediately subsequent to Big Bang (the deregulation of the London stock market in 1986). The owners in this play, as one of the characters explains, are the stockholders – the major investors, that is. The product that a company makes is not important in itself. The one commodity that matters is money, and the characters discuss it in terms of a rapacious sexuality. They are high on it, scheme twenty-four hours a day to make more of it. Everyone wheels and deals in this heady and glossy world of brokers, jobbers, oiks, arbitrageurs, white knights and corporate raiders. Everything is exhilarating, slick and totally heartless.

Max Stafford-Clark, director of *Light Shining in Buckinghamshire*, *Cloud Nine* and *Top Girls*, also directed *Serious Money*. In September 1986 he organized a two-week workshop at the Royal Court Theatre, of which he had been appointed Artistic Director. Apart from Caryl Churchill and himself, the group consisted of eight actors: Colin Sell, the musical director of the eventual play; Philip Palmer, who was the literary manager of the Royal Court at the time; and Mark Long from the performance group, *The People Show*. Max Stafford-Clark had been interested for several years in working on a project about rich people and the City, and it was advantageous but largely coincidental that it became possible to organize the workshop shortly before Big Bang.

The most important aspect of the workshop was to try to get to grips with the complexities of high finance. The group spent a good deal of time at the various markets (the Stock and Metal Exchanges, for example, and the London International Financial Futures Exchange) watching from viewing galleries, and, where possible, talking to individual people and being allowed to watch proceedings from close-at-hand on the floors of the different markets. At the commodity markets they saw items like coffee and sugar being sold, and then visited embassies and consulates in order to try to connect the dealing they had witnessed with the reality of the commodities in their countries of origin. At the end of the fortnight the actors performed a short, visually-orientated piece, based on what they had learned and devised chiefly by Max Stafford-Clark and Mark Long, for the benefit of the people working at the Royal Court. It was not certain at this stage that the research would lead to the writing of a play, and the idea was to provide at least the people most intimately connected with the Court with a view of what had happened in the course of the workshop. Within the next few weeks Caryl Churchill had to decide whether she wanted to write a play based on the workshop. She came to the conclusion that she did want to, and then had until mid-February, when rehearsals were due to begin, to complete it. The workshop was shorter than its Joint Stock equivalent, which meant that the writing gap was longer. In the event, this increased writing period was vital. The workshop had begun shortly after the opening of *A Mouthful of Birds*, and it had been impossible for Caryl Churchill to undertake the research with which she normally prepares for a workshop.

Throughout the Autumn she submerged herself in a daily study of *The Financial Times*, making scrap-books from cuttings in order to try to find a way of structuring her thoughts. The succession of take-overs which occurred around this time, and the various scandals and arrests in conjunction with insider dealing opened up a rich, but bewildering array of possible ways of treating her subject matter, and it wasn't until the final three or four weeks before starting rehearsals that the play really started to take shape. What gave her a 'purchase on the material' and enabled her to get her 'head above the documentariness of it'[29] was her decision to write the play in verse. The zest and elasticity of Churchill's dialogue with its frequent use of rhyming couplets enabled her to move the action along at a breakneck pace.

Apart from the flashbacks and the initial scenes establishing the nature of the financial world, the main action takes place within the twenty-four hours from the morning when Jake Todd is found dead to the early hours of the following morning when his sister, Scilla, arrives in New York. The main plot-line concerns the projected take-over of Albion Products by Corman Enterprise. This is presented largely in the form of flashbacks which are given coherence through the narrative function of Zac Zackerman, an American banker who is a key figure in the deal. Dovetailing with this central plot, is the linked subplot of the suicide – or murder – of Jake Todd. It is Jake who brings the Peruvian businesswoman, Jacinta Condor, and Nigel Agibala, the importer from Ghana, in on the deal to buy Albion shares on behalf of Corman Enterprise. Jake's major source of income is selling inside information, chiefly to Marylou Baines, a top American arbitrageur. When the Department of Trade and Industry become interested in his activities, he is not the only person to feel anxious. Jake is the 'loose thread' that could lead to the unravelling of the whole web of financial corruption.

As an introduction to this frenzied, greed-obsessed world of wheeler-dealing, Churchill uses a brief scene from the 1692 play by Thomas Shadwell, *The Volunteers* or *The Stockjobbers*, in which the characters discuss the possibility of acquiring shares in a variety of Patents. It is irrelevant whether these Patents are of use or not: 'the main end verily is to turn the penny in the way of stock jobbing, that's all.' Post Big Bang the market is no longer the monopoly of a privileged élite. Anyone with the ability to buy cheaply and sell at a profit can corner a piece of the action. The prevailing ethos, however, remains the same. There are 'New faces in [the] old square mile', and they, in their turn, are 'Making money with a smile/Just as clever, just as vile.'

There are golden opportunities too for unscrupulous businessmen and women from Third World countries. It is a mistake to imagine that everyone is poor in the underprivileged areas of the world. The masses may be close to starvation, but a few people are very rich indeed. As Nigel Agibala points out in his upper class, Eton-acquired accent, they've learned their lesson well from their old 'colonial masters / One makes more money from other people's disasters.' Jacinta Condor quickly jettisons her holdings in Peruvian mines when the price of copper plummets, and abandons the workers to their fate. She retains her investment in cocaine, however. She ships this to Marylou Baines in New York, and, if she has to agree to contribute an extra ten percent towards the support of the Contras in order to persuade the C.I.A. to continue to help the cocaine to get through, she will still make an excellent profit: '. . . The guys who use it can easily meet / A rise in the street price because the street is Wall Street.'

Everyone in this city comedy of High-Tech greed is corrupt. The poor and powerless never appear. Mines and factories are closed and the workers sacked or made redundant, but all that is offstage. What takes place onstage is both adrenalin-packed and chilling. The three dealing scenes employ a technique of overlapping dialogue which Churchill used first in *Three More Sleepless Nights*, (a short play, written in 1979, in which the characters try unsuccessfully to alter the way they respond to relationships by changing their partners), and then again in *Top Girls* and *Fen*. In the L.I.F.F.E. scene at the end of Act One, four separate companies, each with their own 'phones and trading pit, deal simultaneously, and the frenzied gesturing and furious cacophony of shouted bids and obscenities build into the raucous 'Futures Song' (words by Ian Dury and music by Micky Gallagher) which ends the first half of the play.

Each of the major characters has his or her own individual speech rhythms, and these chase each other in and out, sometimes blending, sometimes scoring a satirical point, through a deliberate break in the metrical and rhyme scheme. The loosely sprung, lengthy verse lines which characterize Zac's speech merge with Jacinta Condor's snappy, jazzy rhythms, or the forceful driving language of Corman, the corporate raider. When Jacinta Condor offers, in return for a financial inducement, to help Duckett, the chairman of Albion, to foil Corman's take-over bid, she picks up the rollicking rhythm of Duckett, and Biddulph, his white knight. The varied rhythms of the language lead to changes of pace in the forward momentum of the play. In the hunt scene, for example, both the words and the actions create the sense of horses champing at the bit, eager to begin the chase. When the horn blows for the start of the hunt, everyone rushes off, leaving Frosby, the middle-aged jobber who is facing compulsory redundancy, alone onstage. He begins a monologue about what the stock exchange used to be like, and the facile sentimentality of the evenly-accented, alternately-rhymed lines is broken occasionally by the freer, more truthful language in which he describes his anger at the changes that have taken place. The final, non-metrical line, 'I'm very frightened', is disturbingly moving and direct. It recalls momentarily Angie's comment at the end of *Top Girls*, and evokes the uncertainty which underlies the glittering facade of high-powered deals.

The conjunction of the dextrously varied rhythms, the stunning energy which the play generates in performance, and the deliberately two-dimensional characters creates a world which is dazzling, speedy and terrifyingly shallow. The riddle of Jake's death is never solved. The British government stood to lose the most if his scandalous activities became common knowledge close to election time, so maybe MI5 or the C.I.A. were responsible. Scilla's chief interest was never in bringing Jake's murderer, if one exists, to justice, but in taking over his contacts, and making 'serious money' in her turn. At the end of the play she blackmails Marylou Baines into giving her a job. The British government pressurizes Corman into dropping his bid for Albion. Another take-over immediately prior to the election would make the City and the government 'look greedy', just at the time when they need to 'be seen to care about the needy'. Corman is unenthusiastic but agrees in exchange for an assurance that the D.T.I. will cease their investigations, and the prospect of a knighthood after the election. The Conservatives win 'a landslide victory for five more glorious years', and the loads-a-money bandwagon rolls on its way.

The greedy, heartless, late nineteen-eighties which Churchill depicts in *Serious Money* have their roots in the property-orientated values, which, in *Light Shining in Buckinghamshire*, preclude the possibility of a more justly based society. The choice of the name Albion for the company that Corman and his fellow bandits try to seize is ironic. The ancient and noble values that the name suggests have long vanished from the face of England – if indeed they ever existed. In *Light Shining* Churchill presents an attempted fulfilment of the utopian yearning for a caring community, and then shows its enforced suppression. The interwoven possibilities in *Traps* lead to the realization of a kind of utopia, which potentially exists within the present moment. In contrast, *Owners*, *Top Girls* and *Serious Money* explore the achievements which are prized by contemporary society. The tragedy is that the undeniable intelligence and energy which the characters in these plays possess is misapplied. The selfishness of individuals and of nations leads inexorably towards the plundered and devastated planet, and the morally bankrupt society which Churchill depicts in *Moving Clocks Go Slow*.

5

Revolt and the Systems of Control

The Judge's Wife, the first of Caryl Churchill's television plays, opens with a still of the Judge lying dead in a wood. The final moments of the Judge's life are then seen twice, the second time from an earlier point in the sequence of events than the first. A young man shoots the Judge, who falls and lies motionless. Then a car stops at the edge of the wood, the Judge and the young man get out and walk towards the wood. The man shoots the Judge, and he falls dead once again. The main action of the play, which presents the Judge at home in the company of his wife and sister-in-law, is intercut with recurring images of his death. Each time this is shown the lead up to the shooting begins from an earlier point in the action.

The opening sequence in the wood is followed by a court-room scene, in which the Judge, now dressed in wig and official robes, delivers his verdict on the accused, Vernon Warren, who is revealed to be the young man who was seen moments earlier in the process of shooting him. The Judge equates revolutionary activity with crime: both seek to subvert the social order.

> Every criminal is a revolutionary. And every revolutionary is a criminal. For they both act in defiance of laws that protect us, protect our property, protect what we in this society have chosen to be. And whether a man who comes against the forces of law and order presents himself to us as a criminal or as a revolutionary is irrelevant. In either case he is challenging our society. And he must take the heavy consequences.

It never becomes clear exactly what organization Warren represents, but his example is 'stirring [the] country up to a new idea of what is possible', and the Judge is determined to use whatever means are available to him to prevent these possibilities from being realized. The government can match any violence that is pitted against it with a greater violence. 'The forces of law and order are stronger than those of revolt'. If the police prove insufficient for the task, there remains the army, with all the weapons at its disposal. It would be 'impractical', but not 'impossible', if need be, to 'eliminate the entire population'.

Churchill's central interest in the play lies in dismantling the Judge's power. The images of his death, which begin and punctuate the main action, make his potential destructibility clearly evident. The fact that the accused is also the Judge's murderer raises questions as to who is the real victim (and of what?) and which of the two is passing sentence on the other. The Judge's words in the courtroom are terrifying, and yet, at the same time patently absurd. In his wig and robes he is a grotesque puppet, and Churchill follows the savage lunacy of his courtroom address with the reality which underlies his trappings of power. The Judge stands passively while his wife undresses him for his bath, and, when she has finished, his 'defenceless' naked body is revealed.

As the Judge slowly dresses in the bedroom after his bath, stills of a young man who looks very like Warren are seen on the screen of a small television set, followed by a film of demonstrators with placards. The Judge does not look at the set. The sound is turned down, and the screen is never seen in close-up. It is 'a small, intense corner of the large, still bedroom', a powerful, but as yet unfocused agent working to blast the Judge's world, and all its values, apart.

The telephone is a further means by which external violence threatens to disrupt the Judge's sanctuary. Each time it rings the Judge or his wife listen silently and then replace the receiver. The fact that it is Warren who is making these calls is established when he is seen, immediately after one of them, leaving the telephone box. He then gets into the car in which he was seen at the start of the play, and drives away. When the telephone rings for the final time, the Judge tells the caller that he would like to meet him 'face to face', so that they could see which of them 'was frightened'. He goes out of the house and walks along a road. A car, driven by Warren, draws up beside him. He gets into it, and the sequence continues through until the Judge lies dead in the wood, exactly as in the opening moments of the play. This time, however, it forms a complete narrative unit, from the Judge's response to the 'phone call, through to his death, and the finality of the event is underlined by the fact that the still of the body in the wood is followed this time by a picture of the incident on the front page of a newspaper.

Throughout the play Caroline, the Judge's wife, is entirely submissive to her husband. Her opinions, which are inseparable from his, are contrasted with her sister Barbara's opposition to the Judge's reactionary views, and the severity of the sentence he has passed on Warren. The two women are both aged around sixty. Their features are similar, but the wife's characterless, carefully made-up face looks much younger than that of her sister. On the day after her husband's murder, she sits on the sofa in her dressing gown, her hair unbrushed, and her 'face crumpled'. She looks old for the first time, as though her true face has replaced the bland and youthful mask. Her sister is also present, and Caroline accuses her of thinking that the Judge deserved what happened to him. When Barbara refutes this, Caroline responds with the words: 'He tried to deserve it. It was his way of committing suicide.' Barbara looks at her sister with interest, but says nothing, and Caroline continues with a long and remarkable speech in which she claims that the Judge turned himself into a deliberate caricature of everything that he had come to detest, but was unable to escape from.

> He wasn't just a right wing bigot, he was a parody of a right wing bigot. Didn't you think so? Didn't you think he rather overdid it? Or did you fall for the whole thing? Did you really? Did you never suspect? No? I thought you would of all people. You're not so bright as you and I think.

Caroline's explanation of her husband's conduct is her way of defeating her sister, a means of getting back at her for her independence, and for the discovery she has made in the course of the play that the Judge once asked Barbara to marry him. She

106

goes on to describe the Judge's realization, in middle age, that he had distanced himself irrevocably from the sufferings of the oppressed, who were 'rising all over the world', while 'he found himself on the wrong side'. He came to the realization that violent action was necessary if a corrupt and unjust system was to be overturned, but he couldn't bring himself to commit violence. And then he understood what he could do.

> He could use his power so unjustly that someone would be forced to take it away from him. He wouldn't kill but he could be killed. He could give his life for the revolution.

Barbara refuses to believe Caroline's explanation and there is a long silence in which she looks at her sister, who remains sitting impassively. Then, for the last time, the Judge is seen leaving the house and getting into the car, and events follow through to their inevitable conclusion. The recurring images of the Judge's death in the wood, together with the telephone calls, and the active television screen in the still bedroom, together constitute an endorsement of the possibilities of change which the Judge strove to suppress. The earlier revelation of the vulnerability which exists beneath his judicial robes is confirmed by Caroline's speech. The motivations which she puts forward for her husband's behaviour are not the true ones, but their effect is to undermine still further the image of the Judge as an all-powerful figure of authority. Though Caroline attempts to defend his actions, she does this through a rejection of the values on which he had based his life. Her speech is a final, and vitally important, means by which Churchill detonates the Judge's authority. The forces of law and order are undermined from without in the play by the revolutionary activity of which Warren is the representative, and from within by the Judge's sister-in-law and in the end, albeit unintentionally, by his wife.

Caryl Churchill followed the writing of *The Judge's Wife* with *Owners* and *Moving Clocks Go Slow*. The latter play was written in 1973, the same year as a television play, *Turkish Delight*, and *Perfect Happiness*, which was performed on radio, and as a lunch-time play at the Soho Poly. The two plays are similar in that they have all-female casts, and revolve round the attitudes of various women to an unseen, or unheard, man. Like *The Judge's Wife*, they debunk aspects of male power. *Turkish Delight*, which was part of a series of television plays with the overall title of *Masquerade*, is set in a bedroom which has been turned into a ladies' room for the use of guests at a party for the rich and famous. A call girl, and the fiancée and ex-wife of John, the unseen man, come into the ladies' room, sometimes singly and sometimes in twos, and talk to the attendant about the progress of the party. Each of the three guests is wearing the costume of an Eastern dancing girl (brief top, bare midriff, long skirt), because this is a major ingredient of John's favourite sexual fantasy. The Ex-wife has come dressed in this outfit in the hope of regaining his attentions, and the Call Girl to remind her ex-client that she knows what he likes and to signal her intention of blackmailing him. The Fianceé and the Ex-wife discuss what the Call Girl is up to, and decide to co-operate in order to stop her.

The last time the women enter, the three of them are together, and the Call Girl's nose is bloody because the Fianceé has hit her. Members of the press who are present at the party start to bang on the door in the hope of getting a story. The women barricade it, and, in the process of discussing their relationships with John, come to the conclusion that they no longer want to be 'Turkish Delights'. They hunt around for new fancy dresses to wear, and the Call Girl decides to be 'something from a horror film.' She wraps herself in a sheet and spreads the blood from her nose around her face. The Fianceé winds toilet paper round the Ex-wife to turn her into an Egyptian mummy, and then takes off her own clothes to become Lady Godiva. At the last moment she realizes that the other guests might think she's just herself without clothes on, but decides that it doesn't matter. In the characters of their new, self-determined identities, the three ex-Turkish Delights go back into the party.

The setting for *Perfect Happiness* is Felicity's kitchen, where she is baking a cake, and talking to two young women, Leanne and Margo, who work in her husband's office. At the age of thirty-five, Felicity has had 'ten years of perfect happiness' with Geoffrey. Unfortunately, however, he failed to come home the previous night, and, in between explaining how to bake the perfect cake and every aspect of being an ideal wife, Felicity tries to discover whether he is sexually involved with Leanne or Margo. She professes disbelief when the two of them criticize Geoffrey and claim not to have found him particularly attractive, but her confidence is finally shaken when they explain, in circumstantial detail, how Margo shot him, one night when they were working late at the office. It happened, she explains, because Geoffrey was excited by the close proximity of girls and guns. He handed the weapon to her, and she thought at first of the power this gave her to make Geoffrey do whatever she wanted, but then she decided to shoot him instead. With Leanne's help, she put the body in a large, plastic rubbish bag, and the two of them took it by bus to Westminster Bridge, where they tipped it into the river.

Felicity's hands are shaking too much by the end of this recital of events to get the cake out of the oven. As Margo takes it out, they see Geoffrey's car drawing up outside, and Geoffrey getting out of it and coming towards the house. Felicity's relief, when she discovers that the murder was a fabrication, is followed by the realization that she still doesn't know where Geoffrey spent the night, or what his relationship actually is with either of the women. Leanne and Margo decide not to stay to hear Geoffrey's explanations. As they leave, Felicity calls after them that there is more to Geoffrey and herself than they think.

Like Caroline in *The Judge's Wife*, Felicity is confronted with a view of her husband which conflicts with her own. Margo, and Leanne, the self-styled 'domestic guerrilla', are the counterparts of the telephone calls and pictures on the television screen in the earlier play. They infiltrate Felicity's snug, smug existence, and do their best to explode it.

In *Objections to Sex and Violence*, written in 1974, Churchill returns for her subject matter to the revolutionary activity of Vernon Warren in *The Judge's Wife*, but the focus this time is on the reasons against violent acts of protest. Once again, there are two sisters of strongly opposed views, although, in this play, they are young. There is also an older woman, who achieves a fairly radical readjustment of her former attitudes.

Objections to Sex and Violence was the first of Churchill's plays to receive a main stage production at the Royal Court Theatre (January 1975). The action takes place on a beach in the fitful sunshine of an English June day, and the focus of the title's objections is a young woman called Jule, whose liberated sexuality, and belief in anarchistic violence as a legitimate form of social protest is disapproved of, for a variety of reasons, by the other characters. Jule, and the two men and one woman with whom she lives, have been arrested, ostensibly on a charge of possessing cannabis, but in reality on suspicion of being involved in terrorist activities. At the beginning of the play, Jule and a man named Eric have been released on bail, and are staying in a tent on a cliff-top. Jule's sister, Annie, has been alarmed by newspaper reports linking Jule's arrest with explosions, and she and her boyfriend, Phil, have tracked Jule down to try to discover the truth of the situation.

Essentially, the play takes the form of a fairly loosely constructed debate on the theme of the acceptability of violence as a means of effecting social change. Phil feels able to condone the destruction of property, and even to agree with assassination in certain circumstances. ('If Hitler had had an assassin he'd be a hero'), but baulks at 'indiscriminate terror.' Annie sympathizes with Jule's ideas, but is unable to accept the practical realization of them, which leads to innocent people being killed and maimed.

> I've seen pictures in the papers and I can't go along with it, Jule. You see the man's shock. He hasn't been asked does he want his arm blown off for this cause. He has his wife and children and things to do. He doesn't want to take part.

To the objections raised by Phil and Annie, are added those of Jule's estranged husband, Terry, a communist who condemns as irrelevant isolated acts of individual violence, and a middle-aged couple who are spending the day on the beach. Madge and Arthur extol the virtues of obedience and strong government. They advocate sexual and racial purity, and are proud of their son, who is a member of the National Front.

Jule's sexuality creates problems for both Arthur and Phil. Arthur disapproves of sex, but is unable to prevent himself from furtively watching young women on the beach, and reading a pornographic magazine, which he hides behind a copy of the *Daily Express*. Phil has a good deal of anger and frustration bottled up inside him. Beneath his quiet, smiling exterior, he is conscious of feelings of self-hatred at the way he accepts whatever happens to him without protest. Despite his love for Annie, and his disapproval of her sister's life-style, he is attracted to Jule, and furious when she refuses to take his advances seriously. Near the end of the first act, he enters with a can of petrol that he has bought to help with a fire that the sisters have lit. Jule, who is close to the fire, trying to encourage it to burn more brightly, is explaining the need for violence in order to make the rich and powerful sit up and take notice. She tells Phil that he must stop smiling 'yes' to everything, and learn to say no. Suddenly, Phil throws the petrol on to the fire, so that Jule only 'just manages to get out of the way as it flares up'.

This is one of the relatively few powerful visual moments in a play which communicates with an audience chiefly through words. Another strong physical image, this time in Act Two, again demonstrates a sudden eruption of submerged feeling. Annie, who is in the process of burying Jule up to her neck in sand as they used to do when they were children, begins to talk about the envy she has always felt at her sister's confidence and lack of inhibition, and the desire she is sometimes conscious of to hurt her physically. Jule begins to laugh because Annie has been urging her to come and stay with Phil and herself, where she will be safe. In a sudden spurt of anger, Annie covers her sister's face with sand, and presses it down into her eyes and mouth, so that Jule has to struggle to free herself.

The relationship between the two contrasted sisters is one of the strongest elements in the play. In Act One there is a brief, but evocative encounter between Jule and another woman, which brings together strands of sexual need, self-repression, and violence. Miss Forbes, who is aged about sixty, has come to the beach to try to find some contact with a crucial moment in her past life. Many years earlier she spent a day by the sea in

111

company with a man. They lay in the sand dunes in glorious sunshine, and she wanted to agree to his suggestion that they should make love, but was afraid to do so. The memory remains with her as a possibility of joy which has been irrevocably lost. She is a recluse now, and finds it difficult to face the outside world. On a number of occasions she has set off to look for the beach where the incident occurred, but has been unable to brave the terrors of the journey. This time, however, she has managed it, but she is not sure that she has come to the right place. Everything seems so different. It has begun to rain heavily, and she shelters by some rocks. Jule also comes in and shelters, and the two very dissimilar women talk about love and violence. 'Suppose you had the material to blow something up? What would you do with it?' Jule asks, and Miss Forbes replies that she would hold it tightly against her body. She blames herself for her wasted life, she 'shouldn't have ever said no'.

Though she appears only briefly in the play, Miss Forbes is a key figure. She evokes strong echoes of Churchill's other work. Like so many of the characters in the radio plays, she has tried to shut herself off from memories and other lives. Despite her seclusion, she has found it difficult to keep the outside world at bay ('There's so much information you can't keep out.'), and has come to realize the need to find a new relationship with the past. Arthur discovers her weeping by herself in the rain, and makes a clumsy, but welcome, attempt to comfort her. The two of them exchange confidences about their frustrated lives, and Arthur becomes sexually excited and starts to undo his trousers. Miss Forbes runs away in alarm, but later remembers his kindness, when he found her in tears, and realizes that he acted chiefly out of loneliness. The encounter with Arthur, and the sympathy which she comes to feel for him, enables her to forgive the man in her past, and, like the central character in *Henry's Past*, to find a more constructive relationship with the present moment.

Miss Forbes makes the most substantial change in the course of the play. There are small adjustments as far as the other characters are concerned, but Jule's uncompromising stance, and the others' objections to it, result inevitably in a sense of stasis. In the last scene of the play Jule and Terry, who are alone on the beach, talk about what has happened to them since they split up, and about their political differences. They have 'no trouble finding things [they] both think are wrong'. The problem is that they can't agree on a solution. Jule asks Terry if he will stay the night, but refuses to return home with him the next day. The play ends with the two of them sitting silently in the sunshine.

The Legion Hall Bombing, written in 1978, *Softcops*, the first draft of which was also written in 1978, and *Crimes*, written in 1981, extend further ideas on the depoliticization of acts of subversion which Churchill raised in the courtroom speech in *The Judge's Wife*. The third of the television plays, *The After Dinner Joke*, written in 1977, approaches the question of the definition of political activity from a different angle.

When Miss Selby, ex-personal secretary of the sales manager of Price's Bedding, begins her new job as a fund-raiser for various charities, she is determined to remember that 'A charity is by definition nonpolitical.' Everything she learns in the course of her job, however, makes this position increasingly untenable. She suggests a publicity campaign round a poster, with a starving child, and 'the caption, This is your fault', but the idea is vetoed as too political. People want to give to charity, she is told, in order to feel good. There must be no question of blame, of individuals, or governments. The director of the charity describes a television commercial devised by Oxfam, depicting a white hand cutting a slice from a cake, and then taking the cake, while a black hand took the slice, which was turned down by ITV on the grounds that it 'was political'. Now Oxfam are selling a book called *Pass the Port*: 'After dinner jokes by top people. That's far more the spirit.'

Her various trips abroad open Miss Selby's eyes to the fact that a good deal of the money which is donated to Third World countries never reaches those who need it most. She investigates the possibility that there are people in these countries who want a fairer distribution of wealth, but discovers that they are called guerrillas, and their activities are unquestionably political. On a flight to the scene of a hurricane disaster, she learns from a fellow passenger that the reason why so many people

113

have been killed and made homeless is that, in order to grow food, the peasants were forced to chop down trees when the land they previously used was expropriated by commercial banana growers. As a result, 'when the wind and rain came pouring down there was nothing to hold the earth on the hills', and eight thousand people died in an avalanche of rocks and mud. Even an event which had seemed to be an Act of God turns out to be political.

Miss Selby finds herself in a no-win situation. She realizes that, if relief funds are used to rebuild the old-style houses, and return things to the way they were before the hurricane, in all probability the disaster will repeat itself. The only way to effect any lasting benefit is by changing society – and this would be political. When she is captured by guerrillas, she sends a message to the charity director that their 'share of the disaster emergency fund should be divided between the peasants' league and the liberation movement', but her views undergo a transformation once she has been rescued. She decides that she needs a break from charity. The experience she has gained will be an invaluable help in a career in management.

The subject of *The Legion Hall Bombing* is the trial, in Belfast, of Willie Gallagher for the bombing of the British Legion Hall in Strabane in January 1975. On the strength of a confession to the police which he denied having made Gallagher was sentenced to twelve years imprisonment.

In November 1977 Caryl Churchill was given the transcript of Gallagher's trial. She showed it to Margaret Matheson, a producer of the BBC *Play for Today* series (for which *The After Dinner Joke* had been written), who suggested that they should create a television piece about the trial for a vacant slot in the series. In company with Roland Joffe, the director, Churchill visited Northern Ireland and talked to lawyers and other people involved with the case. The writer and director came to the conclusion that the simplest and most effective way of treating the material would be to present a shortened form of the transcript of the trial, with a voice-over commentary at the beginning and end of the piece explaining the implications of what was happening.

From the beginning of the work process the intention was to

draw attention to the possibility that Gallagher had been sentenced for crimes he did not commit, and to examine the role of the courts in Northern Ireland. The introduction Churchill wrote described the action of the Diplock Committee, which was set up in 1972:

> to find ways of dealing with terrorists other than by internment without trial, which was causing widespread disapproval. According to the Diplock Committee it was difficult to get convictions in the Courts, because of the intimidation of potential witnesses and the difficulty of finding impartial jurors for sectarian crimes. They therefore recommended a different kind of trial for political offences, which was adopted under the Northern Ireland Emergency Provisions Act 1973. There is no jury. The judge sits alone. And the rules of evidence have been altered so that a confession is allowed as evidence even if it was obtained by threats or force.

The play was originally scheduled for transmission early in 1978, but was postponed because of the BBC's concern about the situation in Northern Ireland. For some time it was uncertain whether the programme would be shown at all, but the makers were eventually told that it would be transmitted in August. In July the BBC asked for cuts and alterations in the opening commentary, and the complete deletion of the epilogue, as it was anticipated that this would be covered by the discussion that was scheduled to take place after the play. The writer and director refused to agree to these changes, and asked, unavailingly, for a meeting with the BBC to discuss the commentary. Caryl Churchill suggested that the commentary should remain in its original form, but with a disclaimer to the effect that it expressed the viewpoint of the makers of the play, and was not an editorial comment by the BBC. This proposal was not accepted.

Despite the opposition of the programme makers, the BBC went ahead with the proposed changes. In the substantially amended opening commentary the words 'political offences' were not used, and the overall effect was to make the Courts seem a more acceptable and legitimate response to the situation in Northern Ireland. Churchill's concluding statement was deleted despite the fact that the proposed discussion programme was eventually scrapped. In this statement she had noted the success of the 'Diplock Courts' in securing convictions, and queried the value of the Defence presenting a case at all: 'If Courts can accept unsigned statements put forward by the police with no corroborative evidence and reject the evidence of a defence witness without explanation'.

The play was transmitted on 22 August, 1978. At their own request, Caryl Churchill's and Roland Joffe's names were removed from the credits. (Margaret Matheson was out of the country when the final decisions relating to the play were made.) They had considered taking out an injunction to prevent the showing of the play, but finally decided against this. The production had already received substantial press coverage, and they felt that potential viewers would know that it had been censored. The best solution, therefore, seemed to be to allow the transmission to go ahead, so that people could make up their own minds about the trial and the issues involved.

The experience of working on *The Legion Hall Bombing* fed into the stage play which Caryl Churchill began to write in the same year. *Softcops* develops ideas on the depoliticization of subversive acts, through terming them crimes, 'that she had explored in *The Legion Hall Bombing* and *The Judge's Wife*, and links them to an examination of the means by which governments exercise social control. While she was working on a play about contemporary, indirect means of control (through schools, hospitals, social workers, etc.) she read Michel Foucault's *Discipline and Punish*, and the memoirs of Vidocq, the criminal turned chief of the French Sûreté, and her fascination with these works lead her to change the play's setting to nineteenth-century France.

Softcops, which has a large, all-male cast, is a mixture of macabre revue and dramatized lecture. There are songs, mob sequences, an amputation, an execution, and demonstrative sketches which show the central character, Pierre's quest for the ideal form of punishment which will serve as the perfect lesson to the general public in 'civic duty and moral feeling'. Pierre is the reformer whose new attitudes to crime and its

116

punishment are contrasted with those of the Minister, who has happy memories of the days of his youth when punishment was a festival of agony which openly celebrated the power of the state over the body of the offender. Whatever atrocity the prisoner might have committed, the forces of justice had the power to hurt him more.

At the beginning of the play Pierre is 'anxiously supervising' the erection of a scaffold, and explaining the purpose of the various elements to a neat crocodile of schoolboys who arrive to watch the proceedings in the company of their headmaster. The posters and placards relate the punishments to the crimes. A murderer who strangled his employer will be hanged, a thief who stole a leg of lamb will have the hand that did the deed amputated (though, as one of the children points out, it might be more logical to cut his leg off). The use of colour has clearly defined significance. The black cloth which drapes the scaffold represents grief, and the red of the ribbons which decorate it stands for 'blood and passion, the blood shed by passion and the blood shed by Reason in justice and grief'. When the prisoner, Duval, arrives at the scaffold, with the placard announcing that he is a thief around his neck, he is dressed entirely in black, apart from his right hand which is to be amputated, and which is covered with a red glove. The executioner wears red, and the magistrate black. The guards and musicians are in black and red.

Pierre's aim is to balance 'terror' and 'information'. If the Minister is impressed by the punishments, he hopes to be able to fulfil his dream of 'a Garden of Laws', where in the midst of flowers and shrubs, 'there would be displayed every kind of crime and punishment'. Each one would have its explanatory placards and distinguishing colours, and there would be guides who would ensure that the families who came to the garden for a Sunday outing drew the correct moral from what they were seeing. High in the air, so that it served as a focal point not only for the garden but for the entire city, there would be an iron cage for the worst crime of all, parricide. From whatever angle one looked, one would see the criminal hanging there, and 'Quietly take it to heart. A daily lesson.'

Pierre's attempt to use punishment as a rational method of instruction backfires when the murderer, Lafayette, refuses to stick to his prepared speech and part of the frenzied crowd tries to rescue him from the executioner. Vidocq, the criminal and informer who is shortly to be appointed Chief of Police, shows the way forward. What is needed, he explains, is a more systematically organized police force with a strong man at the top, plus a card index system to keep track of all known offenders. It is vital also that acts of subversion should be dealt with quietly, out of public view. When Pierre wants to make an example of a would-be regicide, Vidocq persuades him of the folly of this ('people follow an example'), and, instead, Pierre creates a spectacle out of the execution of a romantic-looking, but incompetent murderer and petty thief called Lacenaire.

Vidocq's methods increase the rate of crime detection, but for Pierre the question of the ideal form of punishment remains. He finds the clue he has been looking for in the experiments of the headmaster, who has perfected a method of control, through a system of signals, which results in instant obedience and largely does away with the need for corporal punishment. The boys' minds 'are fastened every moment of the day to a fine rigid frame'. Pierre realizes that, if he can attach the prisoners, or alternatively the public, in a similar way, he will have found what he is looking for.

It seems as though a chain gang might be the answer, but unfortunately this causes the prisoners to glorify their crimes, and occasions a riot wherever it goes. The solution to Pierre's problem is provided by Jeremy Bentham, who simply and effectively demonstrates the principle of his panopticon, by disappearing behind a curtain which represents a central control tower. Pierre is left sitting by himself, and his growing sense of unease, at being watched by someone he can't see, leads him to reverse his earlier idea of an iron cage which would be the focus of the spectators' attention. 'Instead of thousands of people watching one prisoner, one person can watch thousands of prisoners.' It isn't even essential that they are supervised all the time. What matters is that they think they are being watched. With this new system, punishment becomes secret. It aims to affect not the spectators who attend the public punishments, but the prisoner. In addition it serves as a model of centralized control which can be adapted for use in a variety of institutions: a reformatory, school, factory, hospital, etc. Pierre has the means at his disposal to create a whole city 'on the great panoptic principle.'

Softcops is a chilling play, but also a funny and exhilarating one. Through its demonstration of the mechanism of control, it continues the dismantling of the power of authority which Churchill began in *The Judge's Wife*. Pierre's earnest and myopic search for the perfect system of punishment is both disturbing and ridiculous, and the final scenes contain suggestions of subversive possibilities which could bring the whole panoptic structure tumbling down. In the penultimate scene the use of an informer to infiltrate a revolutionary organization is frustrated when a member of the group pretends to be a police spy in order to trick the real culprit into confessing. Like *Objections to Sex and Violence*, the last scene takes place on a beach. Pierre regularly brings groups of convicts, or the physically or mentally sick, for a day by the sea. This time he has accompanied a group of prisoners who have been gaoled for political offences. One of them tries to attack Pierre, but he is immediately shot by a guard. At the end of the play Pierre, who is somewhat drunk, and more than a little confused, rehearses a speech which he intends to make later to mark the laying of the foundation stone for one of his projects. His ideas grow progressively more muddled so that, in his final description of the necessary treatment of the various troublesome members of society:

> The sick are punished. The insane are educated. The workers are cured . . . The unemployed are punished. The criminals are normalised. Something along those lines.

The play ends with Pierre sitting in the sunshine, drinking while the prisoners, who are paddling in the sea, turn to look at him. The final moments connect with those of *The Judge's Wife*, and *Objections to Sex and Violence*. The latter play ends in sunshine and statis. The former is more active, in that Barbara's perusal of her sister, in context, undermines Caroline's version of the Judge's motives. The question of who is looking at whom is central to *Softcops*. When the prisoners focus their attention on Pierre, therefore, this has a greater disruptive power than

Barbara's action in the television play. At the beginning of *Softcops* Pierre tries to transform punishment from a hideous festival into a lesson. With the adoption of the panopticon, he is able to exclude the mass of spectators, and substitute one all-powerful figure who sees without being seen.

The end of the play raises hopes that the mechanism of control may be about to be destroyed. Pierre's incoherent speech mocks the ideas he represents, and the prisoners' actions break through previously established patterns of behaviour. The representative of authority, and, through him, the methods of control, become, finally, objects of scrutiny.

Set in the year two thousand, the television play, *Crimes*, consists of a sequence of framing devices, which progressively establish for the viewer a definition of crime which includes pretty well every form of anti-government protest, and a set of values characterized by a selfishness that is the counterpart of the acquisitive individualism of *Owners*, *Top Girls* and *Serious Money*. The play opens with a monologue from a young girl called Jane, who describes the murders and acts of arson she has committed, and the electric shock therapy treatment which has enabled her to live in the community instead of being locked up in prison. She has had an electrode implanted, which enables the authorities to monitor her movements. She can also give herself a small electric shock whenever she feels the urge to do anything wrong.

A little way into Jane's speech it becomes evident that it is a video recording which is being shown to a group of prisoners by a criminologist, to persuade them to talk about their crimes. Ron is in prison because he yearns for the wild stretches of countryside he remembers as a child, and constantly strays out of the permitted leisure areas. Elliot, a young black man, refuses to discuss his own case, apart from demanding to be treated as a political prisoner, and talks instead about an elderly white neighbour who has been charged with an offence under the Prevention of Terrorism Act. Her 'crime' consisted in opening her front door and standing on the step. Some local boys were in trouble, and she ignored the young police sergeant who told her to go inside her house and close the door. This disobedience was interpreted as 'obstructing the officer in the course of his duty', which 'is an offence under the Prevention of Terrorism Act'.

The prisoners' responses to Jane have themselves been recorded, and are being watched at home by Melvyn, the criminologist. What is not immediately evident is the fact that his home is a fall-out shelter. Sealed in his underground bunker, safe from the outside world and all possible threats to his personal survival, Melvyn first studies the video of the prisoners' therapy session, and then joins his wife, Veronica, in watching a television programme called *Select and Survive*. The presenter discusses 'entertainment and defence' in the event of a nuclear attack. A wide variety of games will be needed to relieve the tedium of life in the shelter during the shut-down period, as well as a collection of medicines sufficient to treat a range of diseases from Diptheria to Bubonic Plague. The problem of unwelcome intruders is best dealt with by a computerized machine gun which is readily available in kit-form.

During the playback of the therapy session, and the showing of *Select and Survive*, Veronica tries intermittently to talk her husband into allowing a friend of theirs to share the shelter in an emergency, but Melvyn refuses to consider the possibility. He has no interest in what happens to others. 'Other people are going to burn.' He is not. Probably the bleakest of Churchill's plays, *Crimes* reveals a society without freedom or compassion, in which the mildest form of political protest is a crime, and those who are able to do so retreat into privileged and isolated cocoons of safety, while the rest of the population are left to face the possibility of extinction as best they can.

6

Conclusion

I began this discussion of Caryl Churchill's work with *Light Shining in Buckinghamshire* for reasons to which I will return, but it seems valuable first to place the plays, at least briefly, within a chronological context. Like the Mobius strip in *Traps*, ideas weave in and out from play to play, so that it is possible to make connections forward and backwards from a number of different starting points. But there is development within Churchill's work, as well as connection, and the earliest plays, in addition to being effective in themselves, contain seeds which later came to fruition.

The first of the plays to be performed was a one-act piece called *Downstairs*, which received a student production in Oxford in 1958, and then went on to the N.U.S. Drama Festival. It takes place in the main room of a small flat belonging to the Johnsons, which occupies the upper floor of a house. Downstairs, Catherine lives with her father, her bedridden grandmother, and her mentally retarded younger brother. The downstairs family are slovenly and feckless, but the Johnson father and son are fascinated by their lack of inhibition. The mother is discontented with her present situation, and longs to live in the country, where everything is 'clean and fresh'. She is determined to keep her little world inviolate from the filthy, rubbish-filled downstairs, which is spreading insidiously 'like a dark stain'. The son is in love with Catherine, and his mother works him up to such a pitch of anger and jealousy that he goes downstairs and kills her. The play ends with the mother's realization that the memory of the dead girl will always be with them. They will never be able to free themselves from the downstairs world.

Downstairs has clear links with a number of Churchill's later plays. The need to keep one's personal world safe from external, intrusive forces is a theme to which she returns in the radio plays, notably in *Abortive*. Another early, and longer, play, *Easy Death*, which had a student production in 1961, also contains elements of the later work. It centres round two main characters, a middle-aged businessman, and the young man who kills him. Time is fractured in the play, so that the action involving the young man takes place within one day, whereas the older man's entire career is depicted. Structurally, *Easy Death* is a more ambitious play than *Downstairs*. Caryl Churchill continued writing stage plays during the sixties, but they were not performed, and the radio plays were necessarily tightly constructed, and usually short. The complexity of *Easy Death* was something she was to return to in the stage plays, as was its anti-capitalist stance. This is a strain that runs through the radio plays, but it is not until *Owners* that it begins to be developed fully.

The malleability of time in *Easy Death*, and the strength of suppressed, invasive forces in *Downstairs* are central elements of two plays, performed in 1972, which opened up new directions in Churchill's writing. *Henry's Past*, originally intended as a stage play, but actually performed on radio, brings a moment of terrible violence in the past into connection with the present. Throughout the radio plays the characters fear and resist connection, hiding themselves away in isolated places of refuge. Henry comes to terms with his past, and this enables him to live in the present. Miss Forbes's relationship to an event in her past undergoes a similar transformation in *Objections to Sex and Violence*. *Light Shining in Buckinghamshire* and *Traps* affirm the possibilities for fruitful change that exist within the present moment, and, in their varied ways, *Moving Clocks Go Slow*, *Cloud Nine*, *Top Girls* and *Fen* establish vital connections between then and now.

The Judge's Wife, which was seen by television viewers two months before the broadcasting of *Henry's Past*, explores another aspect of Churchill's recurrent theme of the necessity of change. The omnipresent threat which hangs over many of the characters in the radio plays becomes increasingly difficult to hold at bay. In *Not . . . not . . . not . . . not . . . not enough oxygen* images of external violence find their way, via the television screen, into the characters' enclosed world. In *The*

Judge's Wife, the television screen and the telephone allow outside violence and danger to enter the Judge's sanctuary, and to destroy him, along with the stagnant and reactionary attitudes he epitomizes. With *The Judge's Wife* and *Henry's Past*, change becomes something to be welcomed, whatever problems it may present. The alien forces in *Moving Clocks Go Slow* are only seemingly hostile. In *Fen* the Ghost and Val are the channels by means of which external suffering permeates and informs the localized grief and yearning of the characters. Melvyn's refusal to allow any intruder into his hermetically sealed refuge in *Crimes* signifies his lack of compassion, and, in *A Mouthful of Birds*, normality is invaded and set aside by irrational, external forces, with consequences that can be hostile or beneficient depending on the individual characters.

Change, in *A Mouthful of Birds* and *Cloud Nine*, is associated with a fluid attitude to sexuality which has its roots in an early radio play called *Lovesick*. Hodge, the central narrator figure, is a psychiatrist who has developed a form of aversion therapy with which he has successfully treated a nymphomaniac, and a multiple murderer. He is strongly attracted to Ellen, but she is involved with the bisexual Kevin. Hodge decides to use the aversion therapy treatment on Ellen and Kevin, to induce the former to fall in love with him, and to cure Kevin of his homosexual tendencies, but Kevin's brother, Robert, alters the treatment, without Hodge's knowledge, with the result that Ellen becomes a lesbian, and Kevin falls hopelessly in love with Hodge. Like Clive in *Cloud Nine*, of whom he is in some ways a forerunner, Hodge hangs on, for as long as possible, to his view of what the characters are like, but eventually he has to accept their true nature. His friend Max, who is having an affair with Jessica, the mother of Kevin and Robert, discovers that he is happier sitting at home wearing his wife's clothes, while she, in her turn, is only too pleased to become the wage-earner. Jessica has all along been sexually involved with her son, Robert. The play ends with Hodge's description of the way he secretly watched the pair of them as they lay in the garden and looked at each other in wonder.

Alongside the forces in the radio plays which work towards change, there are further elements which recur in Churchill's later writing. Children are an important aspect of *The Ants*,

Identical Twins, *Abortive* and *Henry's Past*, as also of *Owners*, *Light Shining in Buckinghamshire*, *Cloud Nine*, *Top Girls* and *Fen*. The denuded, polluted earth in *Not . . . enough oxygen* figures again in *Moving Clocks Go Slow*, and links with the wasted opportunities Joyce describes in *Top Girls*. The wife's fear, which the husband tries to allay in *You've No Need to be Frightened*, and which is experienced in many of the radio plays, finds further expression in, for example, Frosby's monologue in *Serious Money*, and at the end of *Top Girls*. The secluded beach, which forms the setting of *The Ants*, becomes the location for the debate on violent forms of change in *Objections to Sex and Violence*, and, in *Softcops*, the place where the mechanism of control finally shows signs of breaking apart.

The day after the broadcasting of *Henry's Past*, *Owners*, the first of the stage plays to be performed professionally, opened at the Royal Court Theatre Upstairs. 1972 was therefore a watershed year in Churchill's work, as was 1976, the year in which she first worked with the Joint Stock Theatre Company, and also with Monstrous Regiment. The majority of the radio plays focus on private and secluded lives. With *Owners* a more public dimension enters Churchill's work. The contact, particularly with the group nature of the Joint Stock workshop, was of immense value to a playwright who increasingly synthesizes in her work a capacity to create characters in depth, and to present the wider context within which individual lives take place. At times, as in *Serious Money*, she deliberately creates two-dimensional characters, but, in the majority of her later works, inner lives and public situations are seen to be linked. The interrelationship of characters is stressed, as, frequently, is the interconnected nature of moments of time. The use of overlapping dialogue, and of short scenes in varied locations, are techniques by means of which she underlines the relationship of characters and events.

A further aspect of the growing technical complexity of Churchill's work is her interest in the visual aspect of performance, which goes back at least as far as an unperformed, semi-surrealistic stage place called *The Marriage*, written just before *Henry's Past*. There is a strong visual element in a number of the plays. *Light Shining*, for example, abounds in vivid and haunting visual images: Brotherton and the Man huddled in the cold and wind around their scanty possessions; a woman holding a shard of mirror which glints and flashes; another woman frozen in her attempt to abandon her child; Hoskins holding out the apple; Brotherton as the central element of the Ranters' sacrament of unity. The emotional intensity at the end of *Fen* is conveyed as much through what is seen as through what is heard. Churchill's interest in movement was developed further in *A Mouthful of Birds* and in *Fugue*, a dance piece for television which she created with Ian Spink, and which was shown in June 1988. Based on the reactions of various members of a family to the father's death, it links with Churchill's other work in the way in which the family progress from initial feelings of pain and anger, to a truer relationship with their grief.

My starting point was *Light Shining in Buckinghamshire*, and it is here, too, that I intend to finish. The yearning of the Diggers, Levellers and Ranters for a new and more just society has echoes in *Traps*, the play that was written almost contemporaneously with it, and foreshadows the half-submerged longings of *Fen*. The property-based values which arrest the possibility of a more truly democratic society in *Light Shining* connect with the acquisitive individualism and greed of *Owners*, *Top Girls* and *Serious Money*. Angie in *Top Girls* is linked to Brotherton in *Light Shining*, by the fact that she too is one of society's rejects, but, unlike Brotherton, she is never placed within a context which affirms her self-worth. Brotherton's action in allowing herself to be touched contrasts with the determined and self-obsessed achieving which characterizes Marion in *Owners* and Marlene in *Top Girls*. The hopes for a New Jerusalem are crushed from above in *Light Shining*, but *Traps*, *Cloud Nine*, *Fen* and *A Mouthful of Birds* attest possibilities of fruitful change, and repressive systems of control are dismantled in *The Judge's Wife* and *Softcops*. Though the characters' yearnings are finally left unfulfilled in *Light Shining*, the sacramental union of the Ranters in the penultimate scene releases the forces of transformation contained within the present moment that Churchill celebrated first in *Henry's Past*. It is this liberation in the midst of the enforced restoration of rigidly confining structures which, above all, makes *Light Shining* a key example of Churchill's plays. Overwhelmingly, her work is an affirmation of change and, despite a clear recognition of the selfishness that governs many human relationships, of hope.

Notes

1   *The Joint Stock Book: The Making of a Theatre Collective*, edited and introduced by Rob Ritchie (London, Methuen, 1987), p. 118.
2   Ibid., p. 119.
3   Ibid.
4   Ibid.
5   Ibid., p. 120.
6   'A Note on the Production', *Light Shining in Buckinghamshire*, *Churchill Plays: One* (London, Methuen, 1985), p. 184.
7   Introduction to *Vinegar Tom*, *Churchill Plays: One*, p. 130.
8   Introduction to *Cloud Nine*, *Churchill Plays: One*, p. 245.
9   From Churchill's notes on *Cloud Nine* (unpublished).
10 Introduction to *Cloud Nine*, *Churchill Plays: One*, p. 246.
11 Ibid.
12 Ibid.
13 From Churchill's notes on *Fen* (unpublished).
14 From an interview with Caryl Churchill by Geraldine Cousin. In *New Theatre Quarterly* (Feb. 1988, 4 (13)), p. 6.
15 From Caryl Churchill's notebook for *Fen* (unpublished).
16 From Churchill's notes on *Fen* (unpublished).
17 From an unpublished interview with Annie Smart by Geraldine Cousin.
18 Ibid.
19 Ibid.
20 *N.T.Q.* interview, p. 8.
21 Ibid.
22 Ibid., p. 9.
23 Ibid.
24 Ibid., p. 10.
25 From an unpublished interview with Les Waters by Geraldine Cousin.
26 *N.T.Q.* interview, p. 10.
27 Ibid.
28 Ibid.
29 Ibid., p. 14.

Bibliography

Plays by Caryl Churchill

The Ants, In *New English Dramatists: 12 Radio Plays*, introduced by Irving Wardle (Harmondsworth: Penguin 1968.)

Owners (London: Eyre Methuen 1973)

Light Shining in Buckinghamshire (London: Pluto Press 1978)

Traps (London: Pluto Press 1978)

Vinegar Tom (London: T.Q. Publications 1978) and in *Plays by Women, Volume one*, edited and introduced by Michelene Wandor. (London: Methuen 1982)

Cloud Nine (London: Pluto Press and Joint Stock Theatre Group, 1979)

Top Girls (London: Methuen in association with the Royal Court Theatre, 1982) Revised version (Methuen & New York, Samuel French 1984)

Fen (London: Methuen in association with Joint Stock Theatre Group 1983)

Softcops (London: Methuen 1984)

Objections to Sex and Violence, In *Plays by Women, Volume four*, edited and introduced by Michelene Wandor (London: Methuen 1985)

Churchill Plays: One, includes *Owners*, *Traps*, *Vinegar Tom*, *Light Shining in Buckinghamshire*, *Cloud Nine*, (London: Methuen 1985)

A Mouthful of Birds (London: Methuen in association with Joint Stock Theatre Group 1986; London: Methuen 1987)

Softcops, and *Fen* (London: Methuen 1986)

Serious Money (London: Methuen in association with the Royal Court Theatre 1987)

Other published writing by Caryl Churchill

Description of work on *Light Shining in Buckinghamshire*, in *The Joint Stock Book: The Making of a Theatre Collective*, edited and introduced by Rob Ritchie (London: Methuen 1987)

Select Bibliography

Books

Catherine Itzin, *Stages in the Revolution: Political theatre in Britain since 1968* (London: Eyre Methuen 1980) pp. 279–87.

Michelene Wandor, *Understudies: Theatre and Sexual Politics* (London: Eyre Methuen 1981) pp. 66–8.

Christian W. Thomsen, 'Three Socialist Playwrights: John McGrath, Caryl Churchill, Trevor Griffiths', in *Contemporary English Drama: Stratford-upon-Avon Studies 19*, associate editor C. W. E. Bigsby (London: Edward Arnold 1981) pp. 157–75.

Helene Keyssar, *Feminist Theatre* (Basingstoke and London: Macmillan 1984) pp. 77–101.

Michelene Wandor, *Carry on, Understudies: Theatre and Sexual Politics* (London: Routledge and Kegan Paul 1986) pp. 167–74.

David Ian Rabey, 'Past Imperfects and Present Indicatives', in *British and Irish Political Drama in the Twentieth Century*, (Basingstoke and London: Macmillan 1986) pp. 188–208.

Michelene Wandor, *Look Back in Gender: Sexuality and the Family in Post-War British Drama* (London: Methuen 1987) pp. 119–25.

Colin Chambers and Mike Prior, *Playwrights' Progress: Patterns of Postwar British Drama*, (Oxford: Amber Lane Press, 1987) pp. 189–98.

Articles

Alisa Solomon, 'Witches, Ranters and the Middle Class: The Plays of Caryl Churchill', in *Theater*, 1981 Spring, 12 (2), pp. 49–55.

Ruby Cohn, 'Modest Proposals of Modern Socialists', in *Modern Drama*, 1982 Dec., 25 (4), pp. 457–63.

Helene Keyssar, 'The Dramas of Caryl Churchill: The Politics of Possibility', in *Massachusetts Review: A Quarterly of Literature, the Arts and Public Affairs*, 1983 Spring, 24 (1), pp. 198–216.

Elin Diamond, 'Refusing the Romanticism of Identity: Narrative Interventions in Churchill, Benmussa, Duras', in *Theatre Journal*, 1985 Oct., 37 (3), pp. 273–86.

Michael Swanson, 'Mother/Daughter Relationships in Three Plays by Caryl Churchill', in *Theatre Studies*, Columbus Ohio, 1984–1985/ 1985–1986, pp. 31–2; 49–66.

Joseph Marohl, 'De-realised Women: Performance and Identity in *Top Girls*', in *Modern Drama*, 1987 Sept., 30 (3), pp. 376–88.

Linda Fitzsimmons, '"I won't turn back for you or anyone": Caryl Churchill's Socialist-Feminist Theatre', in *Essays in Theatre*, Ontario Canada, 1987 Nov., 6 (1), pp. 19–29.

Index

133